SHAPING YOUR
FAMILY'S FAITH

One Family's Story of Growing Strong Together

JACK AND DONA EGGAR

PRESIDENT OF AWANA CLUBS INTERNATIONAL

Regal

From Gospel Light
Ventura, California, U.S.A.

PUBLISHED BY REGAL BOOKS
FROM GOSPEL LIGHT
VENTURA, CALIFORNIA, U.S.A.
PRINTED IN THE U.S.A.

Regal Books is a ministry of Gospel Light, a Christian publisher dedicated to serving the local church. We believe God's vision for Gospel Light is to provide church leaders with biblical, user-friendly materials that will help them evangelize, disciple and minister to children, youth and families.

It is our prayer that this Regal book will help you discover biblical truth for your own life and help you meet the needs of others. May God richly bless you.

For a free catalog of resources from Regal Books/Gospel Light, please call your Christian supplier or contact us at 1-800-4-GOSPEL *or* www.regalbooks.com.

Library of Congress Cataloging-in-Publication Data
Eggar, Jack.
  Shaping your family's faith / Jack Eggar, Dona Eggar.
    p. cm.
  ISBN 0-8307-4377-4 (trade paper)
  1. Family—Religious life. I. Eggar, Dona. II. Title.
  BV4526.3.E34 2006
  248.8'45—dc22

                                                                    2006037795

1   2   3   4   5   6   7   8   9   10   /   10   09   08   07

Rights for publishing this book in other languages are contracted by Gospel Light Worldwide, the international nonprofit ministry of Gospel Light. Gospel Light Worldwide also provides publishing and technical assistance to international publishers dedicated to producing Sunday School and Vacation Bible School curricula and books in the languages of the world. For additional information, visit www.gospellightworldwide.org; write to Gospel Light Worldwide, P.O. Box 3875, Ventura, CA 93006; or send an e-mail to info@gospellightworldwide.org.

CONTENTS

Part I
THE MILLSTONE FAMILY: A FABLE

Part II
THE MOSES MODEL

To our four children: Joshua, Justin, Jessica and Rebekah. All grown-up and quickly becoming our dearest friends in all the earth.

Part I

The Millstone Family:
A Fable

CHAPTER 1

WELCOME HOME

———

Exactly three seconds. That was the interval between each violent kick to the back of his airliner seat. Jason Millstone slowly stood, twisted to his left and pretended to look down the length of the aircraft at the rear bathroom. From the corner of his eye, he assessed the young boy sitting directly behind him.

The five-year-old's stubby legs dangled above the cabin floor. With arms crossed over his chest, the boy twisted his chocolate-stained face into a combination of helplessness and indignation.

Jason continued to feign interest in the restroom while he watched his tormentor's red, watery eyes widen with concentration. The short, thick legs slowly rose to the boy's chest, pulled back like the hammer on a pinball machine. The velocity of the ensuing kick surprised Jason. A loud "thwack" signaled renewed contact with the back of his chair.

Not good, Jason thought.

A long, mournful sigh escaped from the man sitting next to the boy. Jason took him to be in his early thirties. Nicely dressed but with disheveled hair, the man did nothing more than stare out the tiny airplane window at the gray tarmac below.

"Get a grip here, Dad," Jason murmured under his breath as he eased back into his seat.

Thwack!

An especially powerful strike caused Jason to clench his fists involuntarily. *Could this get any worse?*

Jason's thought seemed to be the boy's cue. "I want *Mommy!*" cried the boy. "I want *Mommy!* I want *Mommy!*" A powerful piston-like blow punctuated each "*Mommy.*"

Three days of intensive training at his company's headquarters in Los Angeles had taken its toll on Jason's brain and energy level. A sharp, twisting irritation shot through his neck, courtesy of a reckless taxi driver on the way to the airport. Each kick planted new seeds under what had now grown into a kudzu vine of stabbing pain.

Jason could feel himself losing the battle to remain calm. *He's just a kid and the dad's probably dealt with him like this for a week,* Jason rationalized. *The mom's probably sitting at home watching soap operas right now.*

Reasoning that his own wife, Sarah, would handle this situation with just the right grace and authority, Jason took a deep breath, stood up and turned around.

"Excuse me."

The man next to the boy turned from the window, stared at Jason vacantly and blinked twice before blurting out, "Huh?"

"Your son has been kicking the back of my seat for some time now," Jason continued, fighting to maintain an even tone in his voice. "It's going to be a pretty long flight and so I would really appreciate it if you could help your boy find something else to do. Thank you very much." Without giving the father a chance to respond, Jason plopped into his chair. A satisfied grin crept onto his face. Sarah would be proud!

Holding his breath, Jason mentally counted the seconds. Thirty kick-less seconds passed. He began to celebrate sweet success and happily pulled his laptop out of his briefcase. Just then he felt a light tap on his shoulder. Jason turned and found himself looking into the disheveled face of the window-staring man.

"Um, that's not my son," he whispered to Jason.

It was now Jason's turn to stare vacantly.

"Huh?"

"Yeah, I don't know where his mother is sitting, but I've never seen this kid before in my life!"

Jason's prediction came true: It *was* a long flight.

Approximately six hours and two thousand miles later, a rusty yellow taxi jolted to a stop in front of 586 Kearney Street. Jason glanced wearily at his watch. *Five-thirty in the afternoon.* Handing the cabbie a couple of worn ten-dollar bills, Jason slowly pulled himself out of the cab.

A long, luxurious stretch and a gulp of the warm, lazy air invigorated Jason long enough to see the taxi begin to pull away from the curb.

"Hey!" Jason shouted. A feverish run alongside the vehicle and a number of bangs on the rear window finally brought it to a stop.

"My luggage is in the trunk!"

The only reply was the metallic "click" of the trunk latch. Jason's briefcase and black Tumi™ suit bag were quickly snatched from the compartment before the trunk slammed shut, loud enough, Jason hoped, to send a message to the driver. The taxi sat for several seconds as if waiting for any more demands, and then slowly pulled away.

Jason set his baggage down on the sidewalk and gingerly rubbed his temples. His long, narrow frame hunched slightly. He slowly ran his hands through the short jet-black hair that framed his taut-skinned face. Reaching his hands to the air, he stretched his back for a moment. His dark, brown eyes—normally intense and piercing—were bloodshot and only half open. Drained, hungry and sore from absorbing several hours of punishment, Jason's kudzu-vine headache had swollen into a General Sherman-sized redwood tree. He was glad to be home.

Slowly, he gathered up his things and started across the well-manicured, lawn. He followed the curved brick path bordered by an alternating mix of dusty miller and bright red geraniums to the front porch steps.

Even from the outside, the house exhibited the warm, natural hospitality usually expected in the South. Jason stopped to admire the façade. Despite being hammered over the years by inclement weather and errant baseballs, the vinyl siding remained an unscathed expanse of pastel yellow. Several dozen white shutters framed the windows of both stories. The recently trimmed hedges set off beds filled with a radiant assortment of annuals.

Must have rained while I was gone, Jason mused. He took one last admiring glance at his house, then ascended the porch steps, opened the front door and stepped inside.

"Daddy!" A delighted squeal rang out from an upstairs bedroom. Jason smiled broadly as he watched his oldest daughter fly down the staircase. She never touched the final two stairs. Jason opened his arms wide in preparation of embracing this bundle of energy, but she didn't seem to notice. Instead, she dropped to her knees on the hardwood floor and slid the final distance to Jason's feet.

"Did you get it? Did you get it?" she shrieked, already rummaging through his duffel bag. Jason frowned and dropped his arms.

"It's good to see you, too, Jules," he said.

"Where is it?" Julia whined, still feeling around the bottom of the bag. After another fruitless couple of seconds, she looked up at her father with accusing eyes. Sighing heavily, Jason reached down and unclasped his briefcase. The brightly colored compact disc lay on top of a short stack of documents and noteads. The words "Parental Advisory" glared at him from a dark sticker on the cellophane wrapper.

Julia made a desperate pounce for her gift as soon as she saw it, but Jason was too quick. He held it as high as his six-foot frame would allow, while Julia leaped and yelped in front of him like a puppy.

"Dad!" she cried, despairingly.

"I just want a hug first."

A surprised *oomph* wheezed out of him at the impact of his daughter latching herself around his waist.

"Thank you, thank you, thank you!" cried Julia when the prize was finally relinquished. Jason watched in fascination as his daughter turned the CD over and began reading through the song titles.

Julia already showed the potential of becoming a stunning woman. She pushed a lock of her long chestnut-brown hair from her face and focused her intense chocolate-brown eyes on the CD label. *Her mom's hair, my eyes,* thought Jason as he regarded Julia's powder and blush-caked cheeks. A large, pink heart dangled from each of her earlobes. Still appropriately skinny and gangly for her age, the signs of Julia's impending blossom were undeniable.

She doesn't look thirteen, thought Jason with a mix of admiration and unrest. *She looks* . . . "Uh, Dad? Everything okay?" Jason's thoughts fluttered away at his daughter's question. He realized he had been staring at her. He quickly changed the subject.

"What's so special about that CD that I had to drive halfway around L.A. to find it?"

"Are you kidding?" Julia gushed. "This is the new CD from Pink Centipedes! They just signed with a new label, which means these won't get to Midland for about twenty years. This isn't even on iTunes yet! Kim and Melanie will be so jealous."

"Forgive me, Jules. I thought it was a computer game devoted to exterminating bugs," Jason quipped.

"Computer game?" Julia was dumbfounded and unable to grasp his humor.

"Just kidding, sweetheart!"

Julia relaxed but felt the need to justify her CD selection. "Dad, this is a Christian singing group."

"Well, good . . ." muttered Jason, feeling that his efforts in tracking it down were somewhat justified. "What about that?" he asked, pointing to the warning sticker.

"Oh, Dad," Julia scolded. "That just means babies shouldn't listen to it. This type of music is for young adults like me."

A late-model SUV pulled into the driveway, cutting off Jason's next question. "Yea!" Julia squeaked. "Gotta go, Dad!"

"Wha! Where . . ." Jason asked into empty space as his daughter streaked by him and out the door. The passenger door of the SUV opened as Julia ran toward it, the prized CD raised triumphantly in her hand. She hopped in, squealing and giggling. In a second, the car pulled out of the driveway and was gone.

" . . . are you going?" finished a bewildered Jason as the screen door eased itself shut in front of his face. The unanswered question settled heavily into Jason's gut.

"Melanie's mom is taking Julia and her friends to the mall," said an amused voice from behind him. Jason turned to see his wife leaning against the banister. She seemed genuinely happy to see him.

"It's good to see you, Sarah," Jason said. In lieu of a reply, Sarah walked over to him. They embraced, kissed lightly, and then separated in a well-practiced, robotic ritual that took all of three seconds to perform.

At thirty-four years of age and after three children, Sarah retained much of what had initially attracted Jason to her. Of medium height and build, she worked diligently at maintaining an acceptable physique at Bally's gym down the street. Her light brown hair, gathered up into a ponytail, bounced lightly as she cocked her head and focused her emerald-green eyes on him.

To Jason, Sarah's features had been faded by familiarity. Instead, Sarah's gray, faded T-shirt with the word "Army" scripted in block letters across the front drew a frown. Her frayed black britches cut off just below the knees were stained with white and yellow paint. He glanced from her questioning face to the framed wedding photo hanging on the wall, struck by how much older she looked now.

"Is something the matter?" asked Sarah. Once again, Jason had been caught staring, and once again he was ready with a quick reply.

"You didn't think Julia should stick around for a little while?" he asked, glancing back at the empty driveway. Sarah shrugged her shoulders.

"It's Friday night," she said a bit defensively. "Do you really want to deal with her attitude if we force her to stay in?"

"I guess you're right," Jason capitulated with a sigh.

"The casserole is in the oven," Sarah continued. "I'm going for a little run before dinner. Okay?" There was a strained edge to her voice.

"Okay," answered Jason with resignation. As Sarah jogged out the front door, Jason picked up his bags and walked down the short hallway to the kitchen. He turned right at the first door and set his luggage inside the master bedroom. Jason then walked back to the left of the kitchen and peeked into the living room.

The narrow room held a plush, black leather couch placed parallel to a set of vibrant bay windows. A large-screen TV with DVD and surround-sound hardware dominated the entertainment center. Two La-Z-Boy recliners flanked the couch.

An unsuspecting alien from another planet who happened to pass by would immediately recognize this room as the family worship center. Upon further investigation, the alien would discover that Americans all across the country collectively share this particular custom: a black box, placed strategically in countless dwellings, captures and dominates the eyes and brains of all who enter. The Jason Millstone Family was no exception.

The armrest of the couch supported a seven-year-old boy, who was playing an impressively realistic video game. The boy had inherited his father's obsidian hair, and—from the looks of his big, floppy feet—would eventually inherit his father's height. "He's gonna be one handsome-looking guy," Jason had confided to several relatives and friends of the family during the past year. Strangely, however, he had not communicated this prognostication to his son.

Jason noted that the object of the game seemed to be to use a '57 Chevy to chase down and run over fleeing pedestrians.

At the far end of the room, a nine-year-old girl sat on a high-backed office chair in front of a tall computer desk. She alternated between staring first at the nineteen-inch flat screen monitor in front of her and typing furiously on a silver, wireless keyboard.

"Hi, kids!" Jason called as he walked into the room.

"Hey, Dad," came the unison reply. Neither of the children looked up.

"Can you turn that off please, Jeremy?" Jason asked his son. "I need to catch some sports."

"But I'm in the middle of my game!" the little boy moaned, cradling the controller against his chest with eyes still fixed on the screen.

"Yeah, well, I'm your father," Jason chided. He moved in front of the television in an effort to capture his son's attention. "Besides, you can play the same thing on your GameBoy."

After muttering "Fine!" the boy switched off the game system and ran out of the room. In a few moments he returned, holding his GameBoy in front of his face and began furiously punching buttons with his thumbs. Still in a huff, Jeremy flopped into the recliner to the right of the couch, opposite the one that now held the reclining figure of his father.

"What are you up to, Paige?" Jason asked after finding a Texas Rangers game on ESPN2.

"Just chatting," answered the young girl at the computer desk. Although only nine years old, her face had a studious, serious bearing. Her dark brown hair was tangled up into pigtails and her mouth was pursed into a small O of concentration. Her mother's eyes, though imprisoned by a thick pair of glasses in stylish frames, shone with the unmistakable light of intelligence and determination.

"Who are you chatting with?" her father continued.

"Friends."

"Friends from school?"

"Just friends."

The ambiguity of this reply did not alarm Jason. He was happy to be home, and without further delay, he surrendered himself to the couch, the game and his family. Within seconds he was sound asleep.

* * *

Stretches of silence hung heavily in the air as the Millstone family sat at the rectangular table for dinner. Jason stared vacantly past the peas he had picked out of the tuna casserole. His thoughts on baseball, he did not notice Jeremy slowly and methodically separating his peas into a pile just as his father had done.

Sarah noticed but decided to bite her tongue. She had learned to choose her battles carefully. *At least they're eating the rest of it*, she mused.

Paige focused entirely on her meal. Her face hovered within two inches of her plate as she shoveled food into her mouth, stopping only occasionally for a great gulp of Mountain Dew.

"Did anything interesting happen in Los Angeles?" Sarah asked in an attempt to jump-start a family conversation.

"Not really," Jason returned. "Just a few average days for an average Joe." Sarah smiled weakly at Jason's reluctance to engage, and turned to her son.

"Jeremy, how was school today? Anything fun happen?"

"Not really," Jeremy said. Before Sarah could pose her unanswered question to Paige, a huge, inspired smile burst across her son's face. Looking expectantly at his father, the boy cried, "Just an average day for an average Joe!"

Jason ignored his son's attempt at imitation. "Have you brought your spelling averages up?" he asked.

"It's hard!" sighed the boy. He lowered his head and began picking at the rest of his meal.

"Can I help?" Jason asked. He flashed the boy a brief, unnoticed smile, then renewed his segregation of peas.

"Sure!" The thought of actually spending time with his father made even spelling sound acceptable.

"May I be excused?" asked Paige, speaking for the first time at the meal. She held her spotless plate in front of her in support of her request. Sarah began to shake her head in disapproval.

"Sure thing, honey," said Jason.

"Me too?" asked Jeremy.

"Yes, you may," Jason replied cheerfully. The two children sprinted in the direction of the living room. "Good job finishing your dinners!" he called to the children's backs.

"What is the matter with you?" Sarah whispered fiercely once she determined the kids were out of hearing range.

"What are you talking about?" Instinctively, Jason dropped his fork, sat upright and folded his arms across his chest.

"You should be spending time with your kids; *that's* what's wrong!" cried Sarah, instinctively raising her voice in an effort to penetrate his defenses. "You haven't seen them for almost a week!"

Jason took a breath before responding. "First of all, I've only been gone four days. Second, I spent some great time with the kids while you were out on your little run."

"Falling asleep in front of the TV is not quality time!"

"I didn't fall asleep! I . . ." The high-pitched wail of a telephone cut off Jason's rising voice. "That's probably Mom," Sarah said in exasperation. She gave her hair a frustrated flip and retreated to the kitchen. With a heavy sigh, Jason pushed his mostly full plate forward and rose from the table to head for the living room. *At least I can catch the end of the Rangers game,* he thought to himself.

Moments later a frantic tapping on his shoulder interrupted Jason's concentration on the television screen. Turning around, he saw that his wife's normally pleasant face had turned pale. Her eyes showed fear. Sarah motioned for him to follow her into the kitchen.

"What's wrong?" he asked when they were standing safely in front of the fridge. "Who was on the phone?"

"The police!" moaned Sarah. Tears spilled down her cheeks as she lost the fight to hold them back.

"What?" gasped Jason. "Is everything okay?" Sarah shook her head as great, heaving sobs choked any words she tried to say.

"It's Julia," she blurted between sobs. "She was cau . . ." A shudder racked her body, as if in rebellion against what she was about to say. Jason pulled her close and held her until she could blurt out, "She was caught shoplifting!"

Within twenty minutes, Jason and Sarah found themselves half-walking, half-running into the Sunglass Hut at the north end of Midland Mall. The lone clerk recognized their distress and directed them into a small room. Before going in, Sarah saw the cashier shake his shaggy head in disgust.

Inside the room, a large man dressed in a shirt and tie that appeared to be one size too small sat behind a small metal desk to the right of the door. A female police officer stood to the left of the desk. Both of them stared at a young girl defiantly perched on an office chair in front of them.

"Julia!" Sarah cried out, rushing to her firstborn. The young girl stood up slowly, allowing herself to be enveloped in her mother's arms.

Jason searched his mental databank for something to say. The only thing that came to mind was banter from an old television police show. "We are her parents. Is there a problem, officer?" he asked weakly. Instead of answering, the officer looked toward the store manager.

"I'm afraid so," he said, addressing Jason and Sarah full on. "Our clerk caught your daughter and her friend attempting to shoplift an expensive pair of sunglasses."

"They were trying to hide them inside their Coke cups," the police officer added.

As Jason continued to search for an appropriate response, Sarah pushed her daughter to arm's length and demanded, "Where's Melanie and her mother?"

"We sent Mrs. Jones and the other girls home," said the officer. "We thought it would be best to talk to the girls' families separately." Sarah felt hot tears welling up once again. "Are you sure she did it?" Jason asked the manager. "I mean, do you have any proof?"

The store manager gave a knowing smile and pointed to a small, plastic television monitor on the corner of his desk. "Caught it on tape," he said. "I can play it for you if you wish." One look into his daughter's face convinced Jason that it would not be necessary. He shook his head.

"Oh God!" Sarah whimpered, surrendering to the tears once again. She turned to the police officer. "She's never done anything like this before. She's a good girl!"

"Mrs. Millstone . . ." began the officer.

Sarah's initial anxiety suddenly morphed into a smoldering, sickening embarrassment.

"I'm so sorry," she sobbed to the store manager. "We'll do whatever it takes to pay you back. Please . . ." Sarah fought through another full-body shudder that threatened to silence her. "We've done our best to bring our kids up the right way! We'll make sure it never happens again!"

Now Jason, at her side, placed his hand against the small of her back. Sarah looked up at him with a child-like expression of her own.

"It will be okay, Sarah. It's going to be okay."

The police officer and store manager exchanged knowing looks. The store manager nodded, and the officer addressed Jason. "Mr. Chambers would like to consider whether or not he should press charges against your daughter."

Jason gripped his wife tighter as another tremor shook her body. She looked up and listened meekly.

"I'll give you a call tomorrow to let you know what he decides. You can take your daughter and go home now."

"Thank you, officer," Jason said quietly. He turned to the store manager, hand extended. "We're very sorry about this, sir."

Mr. Chambers gave a final glance at Julia, who insolently chewed her upper lip, and shook Jason's hand. "I'm sure we'll get it figured out," he said.

Silence reigned in the Millstone's Honda Accord for the first five minutes of the ride home. Julia propped her head disconsolately against the window in the back seat. Sarah sat next to her husband in the front seat, her head lowered and her hands folded in her lap. Every few moments, she dabbed at the corners of her eyes with a balled-up tissue. Jason stared straight ahead at the road in front of him.

"Do you have anything to say for yourself?" Sarah finally asked, breaking the silence. A stubborn silence from the back seat was her reply.

"Julia, I need an answer." Sarah's voice, still calm, was barely under control. "I need you to tell me why you would do such
a thing."

Nothing. Silence. Sarah turned around, and then emitted a
surprised, enraged squawk. Reaching back, she jerked at the
thin, white wire in front of Julia's chest, pulling a small pair of
earphones roughly out of her daughter's ears.

"Ow! Mom!" cried Julia, rubbing the sides of her head.

"Give me the iPod," Sarah demanded. Any remaining anxiety had departed, any embarrassment had vanished—only
the steady, seething anger of a loving but frightened mother
remained. Sarah would not be ignored. Julia understood and
handed over the iPod without further argument.

"You won't be seeing this for a long, long time," Sarah promised, stuffing the mp3 player into her purse.

"Why?" whined Julia,

"Why?" Sarah retorted. "Why? How can you ask me why after
what you've done?"

"It's not that big of a deal, Mom," Julia responded, picking
up a little anger of her own.

"Honey," Sarah began, more softly this time. She conscious-
ly tried to calm herself. "Don't you understand what you did
tonight? You took something that wasn't yours. That's stealing."

"Did you see how many pairs of sunglasses they had in
that store?" Julia shot back. "They wouldn't have missed two
lousy pairs."

Sarah looked over at her husband for help. Jason continued
to stare straight ahead.

"Besides," Julia continued, "me and Melanie just wanted to
see if we could do it. We would've given them back if we hadn't
got caught."

"Oh, yes, right," Sarah said, rolling her eyes and throwing
up her hands. "It was all just a little science experiment. Okay.
Case closed. All is forgiven."

"What-EV-er," Julia muttered back, breaking the word into distinct syllables. With a sigh worthy of high drama, she turned her head to look out the window.

"Don't you have *anything* to say, Jason?" Sarah asked her stoic husband as the car pulled into the driveway. Once they came to a stop in the garage, Jason adjusted the rearview mirror so that he could see his daughter's face.

"I'm very disappointed in you," he said, holding her eyes with his own. Then he pushed the mirror back, opened the door and got out.

"What-EV-er," Julia repeated. Before Julia could turn to find the door latch, Sarah noticed the silver refraction of a tear on her daughter's cheek.

"Julia," Jason called ahead to his daughter as she walked briskly toward the entrance to the house. At the sound of her father's voice, Julia turned to see her parents standing side by side.

"You're grounded," he said.

"How long?"

"Your mother and I will discuss this more, but don't plan on any outings with your friends for at least a month."

"What?" she shrieked. "That's totally unfair. You can't do that to me!"

"I can," Jason answered through clenched teeth. The muscles in his jaw danced like ripples over the surface of a lake.

A cry of furious disgust split the evening air. "You're the worst parents in the world!" Julia turned and disappeared into the house.

Sarah and Jason entered the house several seconds later just as an upstairs bedroom door slammed shut.

* * *

A little more than an hour later, Jason and Sarah lay in their bed—both were wide awake. Neither was assured of getting any rest despite being physically drained and mentally exhausted.

"You know what the worst thing is?" Sarah asked into the darkness. "It was like she didn't even think she had done anything wrong."

"I know what you mean," Jason said. "The only thing she regretted was getting caught." He paused a moment. "And getting grounded."

"Actually," Sarah remarked, "she was upset when you told her you were disappointed. I saw her cry a little before I got out of the car."

"Huh," Jason grunted, genuinely surprised. "I guess that's something."

"I guess," Sarah answered. After a moment's reflection, she shook her head.

"But how could something like this happen?"

"How could our little girl *steal*?" Jason thought he should do something to comfort his wife, but wasn't sure what to do. After some thought, he reached out his hand and stiffly patted her upper arm.

"Yes?" she said.

"What?" Jason asked.

"You tapped me. What did you want?"

"Oh," Jason stammered, "I was just being . . . comforting."

"Oh," Sarah said, sounding uncomforted and thinking, *Why don't they offer a course for husbands on comforting wives by gently caressing?*

"Maybe Melanie's a bad influence," Jason suggested, desperate to regain the topic at hand.

"I don't think so," Sarah mused, shaking her head again. "I mean, she's active in the youth group."

"Well, so is Julia," Jason countered. They pondered the implication of this revelation in silence until Jason broke it. "Maybe that's the problem," he said.

"The youth group?" Sarah asked, incredulous.

"Isn't that where kids are supposed to learn right from wrong? I mean, it's not like Julia hasn't been involved with the church. We've been taking her ever since she was a toddler."

"That's true," Sarah conceded.

"Somebody's gotta be dropping the ball somewhere if she doesn't even realize that what she did was wrong, right? I mean, that's one of the big commandments. 'Thou shalt not steal.'"

"But Jeff and Susan are such good youth leaders," Sarah protested.

"Really?" Jason asked. "Do we know that for sure? Have you ever heard one of Jeff's lessons?"

"No," Sarah admitted with a sigh. "I guess I'm not sure what goes on there."

"Well," Jason declared, "I think it's about time we have a talk with Pastor David and find out what's going on. After all, isn't the church responsible for the spiritual development of our children?"

Jason and Sarah eventually slipped into an exhausted sleep, their restless minds and wounded hearts bordering on despair.

CHAPTER 2

FAMILY MEETING

⸺

The warm summer air hung heavy. It was Saturday morning and a group of young girls clad in black shorts and red shirts glared southward across the suburban battlefield at their opponents, sporting white shorts and green shirts. Between them lay a black-and-white soccer ball. The battle lines were drawn.

The piercing shrill of the referee's whistle renewed the battle. Squeals of delight and frustration accompanied the sight of gangly nine- and ten-year-old girls scrambling and sprinting after a ball that seemed unable to make up its mind which direction to go.

The girls were not alone.

Two large flocks of parents gathered near the eastern and western sidelines to watch the drama unfold. Jason and Sarah Millstone sat in lawn chairs among the eastern flock. Their faces, a combination of encouragement and strain, pointed in the direction of a gangly collection of limbs in green shorts that wobbled unsteadily beneath the southern goal.

"Go, Paige!" Sarah cried, clapping her hands. Jason inserted his index fingers into the front of his mouth and produced a long, shrill whistle.

"Guard that goal!" he added with a faint hint of uncertainty.

Emerging from the northern pack of girls, a tall, svelte preteen with burgundy pigtails knifed across the field, intercepting the ball from her green-shirted opponent. Four deft taps, three long strides and a sidelong kick sent the ball rocketing over the grass and toward the corner of the goal. Reacting two seconds too late, Paige dove. The leather sphere lay inside the netting as Paige crashed to the ground where the ball had long ago crossed the goal line.

"Darn it!" Jason cried in a terse, passionate whisper. He clapped his hands together three times as Sarah cooed soothing, encouraging words. "That's okay, Paige," he said, as much to himself as to the girl rising and brushing herself off. "We'll get the next one."

Standing nearby, a stubby man with dark pinpoint eyes stared through thick glasses and threw up his arms. Jason couldn't help but notice that the sunburned bald spot on the top of the man's head combined with his long, hooked nose to create a vulture-like caricature.

"Cuh-huhm AW-hon!" he croaked in a thick drawl, adding extra syllables to the two words of frustration. "Thay-at's the third go-all this hay-alf!"

"Hey, watch yourself, bud . . ." Jason muttered to himself. A sudden flurry of activity snapped his attention back to the field. Another red-shirted princess had grabbed the ball and streaked directly at his daughter.

"Come on, Paige . . . please!" Jason half whispered, half prayed.

His prayer was answered. The black-shorted Amazon stopped twenty feet in front of the goal to line up the killing blow. As the girl's leg drew back, a green-shirted defensive player lunged toward the ball. The blond assassin adjusted her kick mid-swing to avoid the oncoming player. Hit off-center, the ball fluttered like a wounded bird toward the net. Sheer coincidence threw Paige in the correct direction. She crashed to the ground with a clearly audible *oooooph*. A second later, the ball thumped harmlessly against her extended arm.

"Yes!" Jason and Sarah cried together, leaping up and down with triumphant glee. "Whatta save!"

Grinning ecstatically, Paige reassembled herself and picked up the ball. She basked for a second in the glory of the moment and then reattached her game face. She still needed to kick the ball back into play.

With her tongue sticking out of the corner of her mouth, Paige held the ball at shoulder height and arms outstretched as if transporting a piece of yesterday's garbage. She took a few jerky steps forward and dropped the ball for the return kick.

Before this day, Jason often scoffed at people who claimed to have experienced an extreme sharpening of the senses during an intense encounter. He laughed at comments like, "The whole thing happened in slow motion" or "My entire life flashed before my eyes."

As Jason watched his daughter's raised leg begin to pendulum down toward the falling ball, the world around him seemed to expand away. Hundreds of terrible, humiliating images flooded his mind. His stomach descended with the ball, a sick, burning weight filling his gut.

Amid mounting horror Jason's senses snapped to full alert. *This is happening in slow motion,* he thought incredulously to himself. Frame by frame, Jason's brain processed the images of Paige's foot landing awkwardly on top of the soccer ball. From the reverse angle, Paige's stationary leg started a slow buckle at the knee. Her hips began a super-slow-mo hula dance and her arms flailed at her sides in a last-ditch attempt of maintaining precious balance on the razor's edge of doom.

After what seemed like several minutes to Jason, Paige finally succumbed in her battle against the forces of luck and gravity. Still swinging her arms, she toppled forward. Jason's internal media center switched from sports coverage to a clip of Saddam Hussein's statue falling forward after allied troops pulled it down in Baghdad. The world then closed back in on him and resumed its normal speed.

Paige's face greeted the green turf one body length ahead of the ball. As the impact wave traveled downward through her tiny frame, her right leg extended and tapped the ball, which rolled gently into the net behind her.

The shrill, piercing blast of the referee's whistle finally broke the ten seconds of total silence that followed this series of unfortunate incidents. "That's the game. Slaughter rule. Edgewater wins!" he cried as he jogged to the center of the field.

The western flock of spectators erupted into a cacophony of triumphant cheers. The eastern sideline remained frozen in stunned silence.

Jason, arms still raised in triumph from the first unfolding moments of the debacle, slowly came to grips with the fact that his daughter just scored the game-ending goal against her own team. In a daze, he lowered his arms along with his head and stared at the ground.

"Poor Paige," Sarah sighed beside him.

"What the hay-eck was thay-at?" cried the male voice several yards to the left. "Thay-at's the most pathay-atic thing I ever seen!" Turning, Jason identified Vulture Man. "Why the hay-eck was she in the game in the first place if'n she can't even kee-ick the bawl!"

A menacing red fog began to swirl around Jason's brain.

"Thay-at's just a per-feck endin' to a freakin' turr-abuhl game!"

Jason's fists closed and tightened as he began stalking toward the vociferous heckler. The fog thickened into a blinding, choking cloud of rage. His lip curled into a vicious snarl as he quickened his pace. Midway to his quarry, Sarah materialized in front of Jason.

"Don't even think about it," she hissed, putting two hands on her husband's chest.

"Huh?" murmured Jason, blinking his eyes. "Think about what?"

"About getting into a fight at your daughter's soccer game, that's what."

"I'm not going to get into a fight," Jason answered, trying unsuccessfully to sound reassuring. The fog was slowly dissipating, but angry bolts of lightning still flashed before his eyes. "I just want to . . . talk with him."

"No way," Sarah countered, shaking her head rapidly back and forth. "This is not something we need to deal with right now." Looking into his wife's eyes, Jason sighed and loosened his fists. His taut body went limp as he took a step backward and held up his right hand.

"I swear, Sarah. Nothing physical will happen." Out of the corner of his eye, Jason noticed his daughter still lying face-down in the grass. "Look, you go take care of Paige. I'll have a little chat with the . . . uh . . . gentleman, and we'll meet back at the car. Okay?" The mention of her daughter's name sent a worried squeak out of Sarah's mouth as she turned anxiously toward the field.

"You better keep your word," she said, pointing her finger and giving Jason one last, wary raise of her eyebrow before hurrying off to console her fallen child.

Vulture Man's mouth continued its flow of disparaging words.

"Hey coach, why doncha just stee-ick a orange cone in front o' the net fer the rest o' the see-ah-son? I garr-an-tee it won't score no goals!"

The pulsing, red rage returned, threatening to consume Jason. Sucking in a deep, calming breath, Jason fought to keep it at bay. He continued in the direction of his target.

"I ain't never seen no one single-handedly lose a game like thay-at before in all mah lah . . ." Three sharp pokes on the shoulder choked off the torrent of words. Turning around, the heckler peered through thick lenses directly into a man's chest. His eyes slowly climbed the figure before him, stopping at Jason's flashing eyes.

"Huh?" he squeaked.

Jason paused. Only now did he stop to consider exactly what he would say to Vulture Man. Inspiration struck.

"I just want you to know," Jason began casually, "that Jesus saved your life today."

"Mah lahf? Jesus?" the heckler stuttered. "What're yew talkin' 'bout?" Slowly the realization began to dawn that bodily harm and the stranger before him might have something in common.

"That's right," Jason continued, with a bit more cheerfulness in his voice. "Ten years ago, I would've ripped your face off for those things you're saying about my daughter."

"Dotter?" repeated the short man sheepishly. Puzzlement slowly blossomed into wide-eyed terror.

"Yer dotter!" he gasped. The man quickly took a step back and tucked his chubby fists under his chin. Jason stepped forward with his hands open before him.

"But I'm a Christian now," he added, "so you don't have to worry about getting hurt." Jason considered adding the words "this time," but was interrupted by the heckler.

"Hey! Yer a Chrees-chun?" he asked, eyes brightening. "Whut church ya go tuh?"

Jason was momentarily bewildered by the man's outburst. "Midland Church," he muttered. "Corner of 9th and Kearney."

"Rilly?" the little man pondered as he took a small step forward. He looked up at Jason with moistening eyes and asked, "Izzat a good church? Cuz I had a lot of stuff hay-appen in the past couple o' months. Dee-vorce an' all that, yuh know? An' I was thinkin' maybe . . ."

"Listen, buddy!" Jason barked, cutting the man off. He did not appreciate this sudden friendly attitude. "I think you're missing the point of the conversation." As the words blurted from his mouth, Jason was immediately ashamed of his hostility. *After all, he just told me of a divorce,* Jason thought to himself.

The heckler stumbled backward several steps. His eyes narrowed into a look of resentful confirmation. "Yeah," he says, tugging his shirt back into place. "Yeah, I get it."

"Hey, I'm really sorry!" Jason exclaimed, wishing he could take back his gruff words. "I was so caught up in defending my daughter that I didn't hear you."

From there the conversation took a dramatic turn for the better as Jason listened to his newfound friend, Donnie, spill his heart out, describing several of life's most devastating storms and their recent toll. They agreed to meet at Midland Church the very next day.

After shaking hands, Jason watched Donnie go and took a deep, cleansing breath before joining his wife and daughter at the family car. Before getting in, he noticed that the metallic Jesus-fish on the back bumper (Sarah called it an *ikthuse*) had been knocked sideways. After a few unsuccessful attempts to fix it, he hopped into the driver's seat and beamed a big smile to Sarah, who had been watching his exchange.

"That's Donnie. He's coming to church tomorrow."

"Really?" Sarah asked in disbelief. "You were red-hot. How did that happen?"

Jason reflected on the incident for a moment before answering. "You know, things are not always what they seem."

* * *

Jason knocked softly on the door of his oldest daughter's bedroom. "Jules?" he called. He did not expect an answer, nor was he given one. As far as he knew, Julia had not come out of her room since they had returned from the mall the night before. Taking a deep breath, he opened the door and entered the room.

Piles of jeans, shirts and skirts lay strewn across the floor. A larger heap in the corner to Jason's left seemed to cover a laundry hamper of some kind. Various jackets and dresses slumped over chairs and the brass floor lamp between them. To Jason's right, two large white dressers stood with drawers open and overflowing. A male pop singer Jason didn't recognize peered at him suggestively from a poster behind the TV. The young man stood on a beach, clad only in a faded pair of blue jeans. The name "Justin" danced in gold letters across the bottom of the poster. A white bookshelf stood next to the dressers, bursting with a colorful assortment of CDs and DVDs. In the far corner, under the lone window, sat a full-sized bed with Julia in the center.

She lay on her back, arms at her sides, dressed in faded jeans and a multicolored hooded sweatshirt. Her body was stiff, her face pointed blankly at the ceiling, eyes closed. The movement of her left foot shifting side to side proved that she was awake. Jason couldn't dismiss her resemblance to Snow White after biting the apple in that ancient Disney animation.

"Jules," he said softly. Receiving no answer, Jason picked his way through the clothes piles to one of the chairs beside the bed and sat down. "I'd like to talk to you about last night. You probably feel I was pretty harsh, and I understand that." He watched her face for a reaction, but there was none.

"Your mother and I aren't trying to make your life miserable, you know. We're just trying to do the best we can to help you kids learn what's important in life." With a sigh, he put his hands on his knees before continuing. "I mean, this whole parenting thing is still a mystery to me. I never got to take any classes on how to be a good father . . . and you know Grandpa wasn't the best example when I was growing up."

He paused for a moment, intending to let his daughter speak if she wanted to. She said nothing, but her foot swayed back and forth a little faster now. *At least she's listening*, Jason thought, and then continued.

"What you did last night was wrong, and your mom and I do have to punish you. But the most important thing we want you to know is that we love you very . . ." Jason stopped as an object next to Julia's head caught his eye.

"Good grief, girl!" he exhaled, rubbing his temple in frustration. Jason reached over and pulled a pair of headphones from his daughter's ears. Her eyes snapped open and she looked up at Jason with a mixture of accusation, indignation and surprise.

"Dad!" she scolded. "What are you doing in my room?"

Shaking his head, Jason pulled a second iPod away from her clutching fingers. "How many of these things do you have, anyway?"

"Just two," she sulked. "I don't think it's fair to take my music."

Jason stood up and picked his way back to the door. "Get down to the living room in five minutes, or you'll be grounded until the Christmas after next."

"What for?" she asked, sitting up.

"Family meeting. Five minutes," he answered, and was gone.

The rest of the family had already convened in the living room. They watched quietly as Julia moped her way down the stairs. Jeremy and Paige sprawled on the couch. Jason and Sarah had pulled the two recliners around to face them. Wordlessly, Julia motioned for her brother to move and then flopped down against the armrest closest to her mom.

"Okay," Jason began, sounding awkwardly authoritative. "Your mother and I have called for a family meeting because we want to talk to you about some of the things that have been going on around here lately."

"Yeah," Paige chimed in, "like Julia getting busted!"

"Shut up, you little worm," Julia hissed.

"Girls," Sarah warned, "we'll need both of you to be civil tonight, okay?"

Jason cleared his throat and then spoke slowly, "We'll talk about Julia's problem later, but first I want to ask you all some questions about how you've been spending your free time. We'll start with movies. Have any of you ever seen a movie called *American Pie?*"

Paige immediately glanced accusingly at her sister. "Julia," Jason asked, "have you seen it?"

After a slight pause, she replied, "Yeah . . . but it's not a big deal."

"Hmmm," Jason said, pulling a small stack of papers from under his chair. "I was doing some research this afternoon and I came across this review." He held the first sheet of paper out for everyone to see before reading it. The top of the review was labeled *Plugged-In Online.*

"Teen sex. Hormones. Titillation. Nudity," Jason read. "*American Pie* takes sex and turns it into sport." He put the paper down and looked at his thirteen-year-old daughter with obvious concern. "Is that what the movie is about?"

After an awkward pause, Julia confessed, "I guess that stuff's in there, but that's not all it's about. It's just a story about a bunch of high schoolers."

"High schoolers?" gasped Sarah, almost unable to comprehend her shock. Paige and Jeremy looked over at their sister with a mixture of revulsion and awe. Julia lowered her eyes as her father continued reading the review.

"Oral sex is viewed as 'practice for the big game' and is encouraged by the only two parental figures in the film. Pornography is presented as healthy for a boy's development and exciting to look at for girls." Jason put the paper down and stared into his little girl's eyes. "And you watched this?"

"It didn't seem that bad," Julia replied defensively. Her voice betrayed a simmering anger bubbling ever closer to the surface. "It's just a movie."

"Yeah," Paige chimed in, cheerfully. "Julia said the second one was, like, 10 times worse!"

"You little rat!" Julia hissed. She reached across the couch and slammed her right foot into her sister's leg.

"Oww!" cried Paige, surprised by the speed and viciousness of the blow.

"Hey!" thundered Jason and Sarah instinctively, reaching forward and pushing their older daughter down. "Cut it out!" With order restored, Jason returned his attention to Julia. "Second movie? Are you telling me there was a second movie?"

"Did you watch the second one, too?" Sarah asked trying to remain calm.

"Yes," Julia replied defiantly, no longer trying to hide anything.

"When?" Sarah demanded, sounding more and more horrified as the conversation continued.

"About a month ago," Julia said, "when Stacey and Stephanie spent the night here." She thought a moment. "You rented it for us, remember?"

Jason was incredulous and turned to his wife. "You let them watch that movie? Here?"

"I didn't ask to see the DVDs they picked out!" Sarah retorted defensively. "And I had no idea what it was about." Then, in a much colder tone, she added, "And you were out of town."

One thing that Jason understood was the fact that his frequent travel was a constant irritation to Sarah. "We need to talk about that later," he said, shifting the subject.

"Fine," she answered, spitting out the word.

Julia hunched back against the armrest. "Can I go back upstairs now?"

"No." After taking a moment to regather his thoughts, Jason turned to his youngest daughter.

"Paige," he said, "do you ever go to a website called *My Space.com*?" Paige gulped. The satisfied smile she had been wearing since Julia was in the spotlight quickly faded from sight. From the other side of the couch—unseen by the rest of the family—a sly, calculating grin slid across her older sister's face.

"Ummm, yes," stammered Paige. "All the kids go there."

"And do you interact with other people?" asked Jason. "Do you ever chat, or whatever?"

Paige nodded.

"With whom?"

"Just friends from school," she replied, "and my soccer team."

"Is that all?" Jason asked again, holding his daughter's shifting eyes with his own. "Do you ever chat with people you don't know?"

Paige shook her head. A silent moment passed between father and daughter. Jason was satisfied that she had told the truth. "Good," he said, "because it can be very dangerous to talk to str . . ."

"Don't forget Walter," interrupted Julia. The sly grin ballooned into a ghoulish, joyless smile. "You forgot about Walter."

"Shut up!" Paige shrieked, leaning forward. Her face twisted into a blend of rage and shame. "Just shut up! You promised!"

"Paige!" uttered Sarah, totally taken by surprise by the change in her little girl. So far, Sarah was not happy about how the family meeting was going.

"Calm down, Paige," intoned Jason, reaching out and placing a hand on her leg. Jason fought to keep his voice calm, feeling the energy of a TV detective wheedling a murder confession out of a suspect.

"Don't you think that's enough for tonight?" Sarah whispered, but Jason pressed on.

"Paige, who is Walter?"

"Nobody," she shouted back, sniffling and wiping a rush of tears away from her eyes. "Julia's a liar."

Jason looked over at Julia and raised his eyebrows. Taking her cue, she answered, "Walter was Paige's online boyfriend . . . before he dumped her."

Paige didn't respond to the accusation. The tears flowed freely, making mini-streams and rivulets down her freckled face. Her shoulders started to shake.

"Jason, that's enough," Sarah said, this time loud enough for the children to hear. "You can't force the girls to tattle on each other and expect them to . . ."

"Sarah," Jason snapped, "let her talk." Horrified at her husband's behavior, Sarah sank back into her chair.

An online boyfriend? Jason asked himself, trying desperately to maintain his composure. *What's a nine-year-old doing with a boyfriend on the Internet?* He nodded at Julia, signaling her to continue.

"Paige started chatting with him about six months ago. He said he was an eighth grader from Chicago or something like that. About two months ago he asked for some bus money so he could come down and see her." Julia turned her head in her sister's direction. "So she sent him fifty bucks with Mom's credit card."

A moment of deep silence followed this revelation. Jason glanced at his wife with an upturned eyebrow.

"There was a fifty dollar charge on our card," she said, feeling sick to her stomach, "but I just thought you bought something on eBay."

Sighing, Jason turned his attention back to Julia. "What else?"

"That's pretty much it," she answered, shrugging her shoulders. "He took the money, and she hasn't heard from him since."

After another extended pause, Jason asked, "Is all of this true, Paige?"

She stared straight ahead, shaking even more violently than before. The tears had stopped flowing, her eyes blinking slowly up and down every few seconds.

"Paige," Jason said again, a little more impatiently, "I'm asking you a quest . . ."

In a flash, Paige's face contorted into a snarl of humiliation, pain and fury. Her eyes snapped open wide, her neck hunched down against her shoulders. Her lips pulled back, revealing white, flashing teeth. "Liar!" she screamed. "You said you wouldn't tell!" With that, she hurled herself over her brother and onto her sister.

Caught off guard, Julia raised her hands to protect herself but was far too slow. Paige snared two fistfuls of hair and began yanking mercilessly back and forth. Julia screamed.

Yelling, Jason and Sarah dove between the girls on the couch, sending Jeremy careening onto the carpet. Jason wrapped his arms around Paige's waist and tugged her away, but not before Paige had succeeded in removing some of Julia's streaked blonde hair.

"You freak!" Julia cried, clamping her hands against her scalp.

"You promised!" Paige wailed in return. She hung limp in Jason's arms, sucking in huge, shuddering breaths of air. "You broke your promise!" Hearing this, something turned in Jason's mind, like a key opening a rusty, old padlock.

"What promise?" he asked, setting Paige on the floor in front of him. "Did you promise not to tell something about her?"

"No, Jason . . ." Sarah pleaded. She had remained on the couch to calm Julia down but now stood up in front of her husband. "That's enough interrogation tonight. Can't you see what's happening?"

Jason was too wrapped up in getting answers. Disturbing answers. He dropped to his knees in front of his daughter and held her shoulders in his hands. "What is it? I'm your father and I want to get to the bottom of this."

"Don't answer, Paige," Sarah commanded from behind.

"Tell me," Jason countered, still staring directly at Paige. One look at her face told him all he needed to know. One look told him that nothing in the world could keep her from saying what she was about to say.

"Julia . . ." she wheezed, fighting back the shuddering breaths that still racked her little body. "Julia sneaks out every Friday night. She waits till you go to bed, then climbs out the window and . . ."

"That's enough!" cried Sarah. She stood in the middle of the room, half-blinded by her own tears, arms raised, eyes wide, chest heaving. "This will not happen any more in my house!"

Julia had crept toward her younger sister, intent on revenge, but the tone of her mother's voice made her freeze. Paige and Jeremy opened their mouths in awe. The only one who didn't hear the panicked edge in her voice was Jason.

"Sarah," he droned, not looking at her—not seeing her stormy, wild eyes. "I just need a couple more minutes. I'm just going to find out . . ."

"No!" Sarah roared, frantically swooping in front of him and sweeping Paige into her arms. "You leave her alone!"

"What . . . ?" Jason stammered, rising to his feet. For the first time that evening, he looked into his wife's eyes. What he saw was pure maternal, protective fear.

It stunned him. It also irritated him. *How could Sarah let such things happen?*

"Sarah," he asked, "what's wrong?" He reached out his hand in an attempt to comfort her, but she backed away with quick, furtive steps.

"This is not the way to handle this," she panted, eyeing her husband warily. "Turning the girls against each other is not the solution. It's only hurting them."

"Hurt?" Jason echoed. "When have I ever hurt *our* children?" he asked, raising his voice.

"Stop it," Sarah answered, taking a step away from him.

"Stop what?" Jason replied, advancing with her.

"Stop this hostile interrogation! You don't know what's going on in our kids' lives because you haven't tuned in to them."

Jason shot back, "You want me to stop asking them why they're watching sexed-up movies right under your nose?" He took another step forward. "Is that what you want?"

"That's not fair!" she moaned. "I didn't know."

"Yeah, I agree," Jason said, nodding his head. "It seems like you don't know a lot about what goes on around here. We've got one girl turning into a thief and another chatting it up with the Lord-knows-who on the Internet. And don't let me forget the sending money part!" Sarah's face contorted with grief, but Jason continued. "Don't you understand that 'Walter' could've been someone bad? Someone dangerous? Someone . . ."

"Yes, I understand!" Sarah cried. "I understand it perfectly. But what do you care? You're not even here! You're never here! It's always work, work, work."

"Don't start with me about my job," Jason growled. "Not tonight."

"Why not? It's true, isn't it? Conferences, conventions . . . this city, that city . . . what about us, Jason? What about your family? I'm tired of you making everything else in your life a priority instead of me and the children. I need a husband and the children need their father to be their hero!"

"That's a bit melodramatic."

"It's true! You're not here enough to realize what I am saying."

"Get a grip, Sarah. I have to make a living." His voice was cool and distant. "I'm in no mood to listen to you start dragging up all that cra . . ."

Something inside little Jeremy Millstone snapped. He began to cry, not in whimpers and sniffles but in deep wails. Seeing his sisters fight was pure entertainment, but watching his parents disintegrate before his very eyes was catastrophic. He could bear no more.

Jeremy's outburst had an immediate effect. The red haze dissolved from behind Jason's eyes. He stooped down to comfort his son, but Sarah was faster. She picked him up and crushed him against her. With one last sour look at her husband, she whisked her son upstairs. After a few awkward seconds, her daughters followed.

Jason stood alone in the middle of his house—his home—holding his head in his hands. A video clip looped through his mind in vivid color: his wife leading their children by herself, alone in the world. The tape played and rewound again and again in his mind's eye. He pressed his palms against his eyes to force the scene away.

"Oh, Lord," he muttered, "what happened?" Receiving no answer, Jason stumbled into the garage, slid behind the wheel of his shiny new car and drove into the night.

After putting all the kids to bed and reassuring Jeremy over and over that everything would be okay, Sarah returned wearily to the living room. She had heard the garage door open soon after she'd retreated upstairs with the children and knew that her husband was not at home. No longer the half-crazed she-bear standing between her children and her mate, she took a deep breath, listened for any sounds that would tell her she wasn't alone and then slid stealthily into the office chair in front of the computer. With a few clicks, she engaged the family's DSL modem and accessed her private e-mail account.

A muffled noise from upstairs made Sarah wheel around to look behind her. Seeing no one, she returned to the screen and typed in her password. It was short and to the point: T-O-R-C-H. She pressed *Enter* and watched as the website refreshed itself, drumming her fingers on the desk in anticipation. A small mailbox icon with a letter sticking out popped up at the bottom of her screen.

"Yes!" Sarah whispered. She clicked on the subject line *I missed you last night*. With a deep hunger growing inside her, she scooted her chair closer to the desk and read the message.

My dear Anita,

I'm so sorry I haven't been able to write. I've been traveling and wasn't even able to read your letter until just now. I must tell you that not hearing from you—not knowing how you were doing even for one day—was torture.

These past two months have been among the best of my life, and I owe it all to you. You're like a fragrant rose in the midst of a noisy city. Just one small thought of you can sustain me, carry me along for hours until I can pause and consider again what a wonderful friend I have in you. What would I do without you?

To answer some of your questions, yes, I do work in sales. How did you guess? And yes, I do enjoy the ocean! It made me so sad to read that you have never seen the sea, as we say. ☺ Although, when I think about it, I imagine gathering shells on some faraway beach with you. You would love it, I know. The sound of the waves, the warm, soft sand . . . it's magic.

I'm afraid this must be all for today.

Good night, my dear Anita (I know you'll be reading this at night ☺). If I'm lucky, I'll meet you in my dreams!
Yours,

Andrew

When she finished reading, Sarah sighed and pressed her hand against her chest. Her eyes were moist with feeling. After a moment's consideration and another furtive glance behind her, she clicked the button marked "New" and began to type.

She finished her letter in less than five minutes and signed off with, "All my love, Anita Brownlow."

After Sarah launched her latest correspondence into the waiting arms of cyberspace, she re-read the latest e-mail from "My friend Andrew," as she called him, and then moved on to other older letters.

She had feasted on the epistles for more than half an hour when a spray of light flooded through the living room window. She looked up to see her husband's car pull into the driveway. With no worry or haste, she logged out of the e-mail server, disconnected from the Internet and slipped upstairs. That night, lying in bed next to her husband of almost fifteen years, Sarah dreamed of finding the man she thought she loved and had yet to meet.

CHAPTER 3

VISIT WITH THE PASTOR

———

The next morning, the Millstone kitchen was the setting for a silent movie. All five members of the family stood, sat, ate, poured, cut, cooked and buttered with the volume turned off.

Sarah and Jason had not uttered a word to each other since the evening before. Mechanically, the salt and pepper passed back and forth between them. Anger was absent from their intermittent eye contact across the table, but they eyed each other with caution, like two heavyweight wrestlers circling in the opening minutes of a championship match, waiting for the other to make a move.

Julia and Paige leaned against the island Sarah had installed last summer. They chewed their English muffins slowly, their mouths moving up and down almost in sync. Their eyes darted back and forth between their parents and each other.

The malice that existed between the sisters had vanished, partly due to the mysterious sibling connection that still bound them together and partly due to a shared fear. Both were deeply afraid of what might happen to their parents.

They had witnessed Sarah and Jason exchanging words before, but never anything close to what had happened last night. They had never before seen that wild look in their mother's eyes, nor had they seen her pant like a dog panicked by an approaching thunderstorm. And never had they seen their father move in a menacing way toward her in the seconds before Jeremy burst out crying.

He looked like he was going to fight her, Paige thought. *Like he wanted to punch her right there in front of us on our living room couch.* She had been thinking this same thought, over and over, for most of the night. A glance at Julia's bloodshot and swollen eyes led her to conclude that Julia had been thinking the same thing.

Only little Jeremy seemed unfazed by the events of the previous evening. He lounged next to his father, right leg slung over the arm of his antique wooden chair. Both of his hands rested against his upraised leg, firmly connected to his GameBoy. His right hand darted with practiced precision toward the table, snatching a large glass of milk. He gulped half its contents, replaced the glass on the table and returned his hand to the control button without removing his eyes from the small screen.

Jeremy operated under the assumption that everything would be all right between his parents—that wounds inflicted by someone you love weren't really wounds at all. He remained confident that his father could fix anything that broke and was sure that his mother would always be there.

Jason again caught the eye of his wife and pointed at the saltshaker sitting beside her plate. Sarah lifted both her brows to acknowledge his request and began sliding it toward Jason with her index finger and thumb. Halfway on its journey, the saltshaker encountered a stray crumb of toast, tipped precariously away from Sarah's outstretched fingers and fell over. The impact sent the chrome lid skittering across the table. A small mountain of salt avalanched its way onto the table.

Still standing next to the island behind their father, Julia and Paige cringed and held their breath. Jason looked down at the pile of white crystals and then raised his eyes to his wife. She stared back. Wordlessly, Jason shifted his chair to block Jeremy's view of the salt. Julia and Paige cast a quick, worried glance at each other and then turned toward the table with their mouths open.

Without unlocking his eyes from his wife's, Jason reached with his right hand and pinched a small portion of salt between his index finger and thumb. In one swift, fluid motion, his hand whipped backward across his body and tossed the salt over his left shoulder—right onto the head of Jeremy, who was still sitting behind him. The salt sprinkled Jeremy's hair and shoulders. Absorbed in his video game, the boy didn't even notice that he had been seasoned.

Jason gave a satisfied grunt as he examined his son's salt-sprinkled hair, and then shot a questioning glance across the table at his wife. The moment of silence that followed was broken only by the faint *whoosh* of Paige and Julia letting out their breath in unison. And then they giggled.

With her eyes still leveled at Jason, the corners of Sarah's mouth twitched upward—first into a fledgling smirk, then into an adolescent grin and finally into a full-blown "good to see ya" smile. Satisfied and relieved, Jason smiled back and let out a good laugh. A tenuous truce formed between them.

"Yes!" Jeremy shouted, leaning forward and depositing his GameBoy triumphantly on the table. "I used my mind ray to stop the aliens from the planet Zeeb from invading," he told Jason excitedly. "I saved the family!"

Jason ruffled his hair, throwing flecks of salt in all directions. Turning to face his daughters, he said, "You kids go upstairs and get ready for church."

Before leaving, Paige shared one last glance with her sister. *Saved the family*, she thought, agreeing with her brother's assessment. *At least for now.*

An hour and a half later, the Millstone family strolled through the doors of Midland Church, down several spacious hallways and into the front lobby. There, they greeted a few friends, hugging and small-talking.

After a few moments of polite conversation and courteous smiles in every direction, Jason and Sarah sent the children downstairs to play in the gym until it was time for the morning worship service to begin. They nonchalantly waited until the coast was clear and then veered to the left to enter the cramped cluster of rooms that served as the church office. Strolling past the secretary's desk, they stopped in front of a closed door labeled "Pastor David Newman."

"You made the appointment yesterday?" Jason asked. Sarah nodded. He balled his fist and reached out to knock on the door, but then stopped.

"You're sure we need to do this?" Sarah nodded again and placed a reassuring hand on her husband's shoulder. With a sigh of resignation, Jason tapped the door three times.

"Come in," a muffled voice answered from inside. Jason opened the door and, after ushering his wife in, sat down in front of an old wooden desk with stacks of neatly piled papers. Pastor David rose from his seat behind the desk and shook their hands.

"I'm glad you both came," Pastor David said while making direct eye contact first with Jason and then with Sarah. *He's so young. What can he know?* Jason thought as he regarded the pastor's short, light brown hair and blue eyes. A wide, unassuming smile fit naturally into the carved lines of David's face, complemented by an air of knowing solemnity. Sarah took comfort in the pastor's calmness, though she discerned that he was a man who had had to learn to be calm.

Turning toward Jason, Pastor David asked, "So, how can I help you folks today?"

Jason glanced over at his wife.

"Well, we've kind of had a rough weekend . . ." Sarah began. She paraphrased the story of their oldest daughter's brush with the law, beginning with the phone call from the police to Julia's meltdown in the garage. Jason mostly listened, offering a missing detail here and there.

When she finished, Pastor David leaned back in his chair and touched both of his index fingers to his chin. "That must have been difficult for you," he said, looking at Sarah. She glanced at Jason and then nodded. "How did the rest of the family react?" asked the pastor.

Jason and Sarah exchanged an uncomfortable glance. Jason coughed into his hand and said, "Well, we decided to have a family meeting." Then, for the first time, Sarah heard about Jason's frustrating monologue with Julia in her room the previous evening. Jason left out most of the confrontation between himself and Sarah. When he finished, the couple looked expectantly across the desk.

"So," Pastor David began, after thinking for a few moments, "you'd like me to give you some advice on handling this situation with your daughter?" The couple glanced at each other in discomfort.

"Well . . . not exactly," Sarah confessed.

Pastor David raised his eyebrows. "That's just as well," he replied, "because my kids are still relatively young like yours and I'm not sure how much I'd be able to help y'all there." Even after three years at a Southern church, David still overextended the word "y'all" like a transplanted Yankee, pronouncing it "yuh-all."

Jason and Sarah glanced at each other again. Pastor David broke another uncomfortable pause. "Well, rather than me trying to guess, perhaps you'd like to tell me what I can do for you?"

"It's just that . . ." Jason began awkwardly, "well, Julia's been attending Sunday School pretty much all her life." Pastor David smiled encouragingly and Jason continued. "And so, I guess it's kind of surprising . . ." He trailed off and looked at Sarah for support, but his wife avoided his gaze.

"Please feel free to say what's on your mind," Pastor David offered reassuringly. "What's surprising?"

After taking a deep breath, Jason continued. "Well, you know . . . it's just kind of surprising how she's turned out . . . morally, and stuff."

Pastor David reached across his desk and plucked a pencil out of a small canister. He tapped it lightly on the desk as he thought. After several moments, he said, "So, you're feeling like the church may not be doing a good job of teaching morality to your daughter."

Jason and Sarah nodded enthusiastically in unison, very grateful to have the pastor realize the nature of the problem.

"Actually," Sarah added, "we also have some concerns about our two younger children as well—Paige and Jeremy. They've been attending Sunday School, well, all their lives also, and we're not sure it's working for them either."

"Uh-huh," Pastor David said, nodding his head. "Well, based on the events you've described to me, it's obvious that something needs to be done."

Visibly relieved, Jason and Sarah let out long, thankful sighs. *I thought this would be really awkward*, Jason thought.

Pastor David continued, "Would either of you mind if I asked some questions about your kids' life at home? I'd like to get a better idea of how I might serve you." Jason and Sarah readily agreed. "Good," said Pastor David, scooting back into his chair. "First of all, when you read the Bible together as a family, do your children ask a lot of questions, or are they more passive?"

Several moments of strained silence ticked by before Sarah mumbled an answer.

"Well, that's . . . I mean," she stuttered, "we don't really read the Bible . . . together . . ."

"Not every day," Jason added after his wife's words trailed off. "We do it mostly for holidays and stuff, you know? Kind of like a special occasion."

"Oh, of course," Pastor David replied, batting away the awkwardness with a happens-all-the-time flick of his wrist. "Special occasions. Hmm . . . can you give me an example of one such special occasion when you spent time with your children reading the Bible?"

Jason and Sarah looked at each other as they both realized at the same moment that the good reverend was no airhead. He knew that their hollow words held no truth.

Sarah spoke up, confessing, "Pastor, we seldom, if ever, spend time in the Bible with our children."

Pastor David released some of the tension by casually stating, "Let's move on to another question. We can come back to this issue later." Jason and Sarah exchanged another edgy glance, awaiting the next question.

"Do your kids do their personal devotions in the morning or at night?"

Sarah swiveled in her chair to face away from Pastor David and toward her husband. She gave him an encouraging little pat on his arm as if to say, *Go ahead, honey—you handle this one.*

"Right," Jason said, tapping his index finger against the tip of his nose as if he had just been reminded of something important. "I'm, uh . . . you mean reading the Bible and praying, stuff like that?" Pastor David nodded. "Right . . . I don't really think they do much of that."

"And why do you think that is?" Pastor David queried.

"They're very busy!" Sarah blurted out, a little louder than necessary. "I mean, there are so many demands placed on them. Just the extracurricular activities . . ."

"Oh, I'm sure they're very busy," Pastor David agreed, smiling cheerfully in her direction. He swung his gaze back to Jason. "So, if you don't mind me asking, are your children receiving *any* spiritual or moral education from the two of you?" His voice remained upbeat as he asked the question.

"Oh! All the time," Sarah squeaked, shifting back to face the pastor. "Whenever they get into fights at home, we always explain that we are a family and we need to love each other, and that it's wrong for them to . . ."

Are your children receiving any spiritual or moral education? In a flash, Jason understood what the pastor sitting across from him was saying. And with that understanding a cold, lead ball lodged itself deep in his gut. A hot, bright burst of shame sizzled across his face and crawled up the back of his neck. The pastor's words echoed inside Jason's head as he listened to his wife prattle on.

"And then," Sarah continued, unleashing a flashflood of parental anecdotes, "just the other day, Jeremy wanted to spend the night at his friend's house on a weeknight, and I really had to put my foot down and say . . ."

Until this point, Jason had maintained eye contact with Pastor David. Now he looked down at his lap instead. He rested his cheek against his right hand and was surprised at how warm it was.

"Of course," Sarah was still going, but beginning to wind down, "we had a long talk with Julia on the way home from the mall on Friday. We really let her know that what she did was wrong. And *why* it was wrong. So . . . I guess that's how we handle those kinds of situations."

"Very good, Sarah." Pastor David was doing his best to affirm her. "It sounds as if you are responding as a loving, concerned parent, but . . ."

Jason jumped right in, interrupting his train of thought. "No, it doesn't."

"Jason!" Sarah exhaled. The flinty edge to his voice made her nervous. "It's okay," she said, trying to sound soothing.

"It's not okay," Jason snapped back, glancing at her. "He's trying to make a point, and we're not listening to him." He returned his attention to the pastor. "Why don't you just come out and say it, huh? You think we're bad parents."

"Jason!" Sarah cried, grabbing her husband by the arm. "He didn't say that!" She whispered the last word fiercely, as though the young pastor sitting behind the desk could not hear.

"Look!" Jason locked his eyes on Sarah. "I'm trying to make a point, and your butting in doesn't help, okay? Why does everything have to be an argument with you?"

"Nothing has to be an argument," Sarah answered. She wanted to raise her voice to match his level of anger, but the energy to do so was strangely absent. Sarah was emotionally worn out from last night and from the last several years.

"It only *has* to be when you make it one."

Then—after several stilted, hitching gulps of air—she began to weep.

The sight of her tears, the sound of those clutching breaths, melted away all of Jason's frustration. His shoulders slumped, his hands fell limply into his lap and a heavy, soggy sigh seeped out from between his lips. In an instant, he also looked very, very tired.

"Sarah, please . . ." he whispered, taking her hand, "Please don't cry."

From behind the neatly organized desk, Pastor David ran a hand through his prematurely thinning hair. He hoped, wished, that this would be the last couple to dissolve into tears while sitting in front of him.

"Sarah, I see that we have touched something painful inside you," Pastor David said, "and I think I now understand what you've been trying to say. Now we have something that we can work on."

Jason and Sarah looked at each other. They were uncertain themselves what the problem was, much less how to articulate their feelings to the pastor.

David began, "Julia has been making some wrong choices. We all know that our choices are generally based on a set of values. Those values—or morals, as some refer to them—are formed in our children most often by the age of ten. By then, a child's moral worldview is firmly set in place."

Jason and Sarah couldn't remember ever having heard this before. Truthfully, they had probably not been willing to hear such things—only now in the throes of a crisis had their hearts opened sufficiently to listen.

"Pastor, are you saying that Julia is acting out of her set of values?" Sarah asked.

"Yes, that's exactly what I am saying."

"Hold on there!" Jason jumped back in. "You're saying that Julia thought nothing of stealing a pair of sunglasses because stealing is acceptable according to her worldview. Is that right?"

Pastor David nodded with mixed emotions. He wanted to shout for joy because Jason and Sarah were beginning to see the truth, but he also sympathized with them over the disturbing implications of such a revelation.

Jason raised both hands in the air. "Pastor, this is the very reason Sarah and I asked to meet with you today," he continued. "How could the church let us down like this?"

Sarah chimed in, "Jason and I feel that the church failed to train Julia by not providing the moral and spiritual foundation she desperately needs."

David sat up straight in his chair. "You know, I need to make a confession and a sincere apology to you."

"Oh, no, Pastor!" Sarah could hardly sit back and let the pastor place the responsibility for Julia's sins on himself. "It's not your fault."

"Please hear me out," Pastor David continued. "I confess I have failed to teach you what the Bible says about biblical parenting."

Jason looked first at Sarah and then at the pastor. "Biblical parenting? Is there really such a thing?" Jason asked, genuinely puzzled by the term.

"Indeed there is," Pastor David said. "Let me show you one passage."

With that, he reached for one of several Bibles on his desk and flipped through the pages with dazzling speed. When he came to the passage he was looking for, he handed the Bible to Jason and said, "Please read Proverbs 22:6."

Jason took the Bible, cleared his throat and read slowly, "Train up a child in the way he should go: and when he is old, he will not depart from it."

Pastor David looked intently at Jason and Sarah and then asked, "To whom, do you suppose, is this command being addressed?"

Sarah squeaked out her halfhearted reply. "Maybe the Church?"

"Can't be the Church," Jason countered.

"Why can't it be the Church, Jason?" Pastor David asked.

"Because Solomon lived long before Jesus, and it was Jesus who started the Church."

"Right on target!" David affirmed with satisfaction in his voice. "King Solomon lived a thousand years before Christ. But my question is still unanswered. Who was Solomon addressing when he gave this mandate?"

Jason wasted no time in responding. "Parents!"

"How do you know?" questioned Pastor David.

"Well, I was in a Bible study on Proverbs years ago and I learned that Proverbs is a wisdom book for parents." Jason could not believe his own words. *For Pete's sake,* he thought, *parents are to train their children. How could I forget this when it came to my own family?* He could only shake his head in disbelief. *Julia was already thirteen! What had happened?*

"Long before the coming of the Church, the Lord providentially established parents as the rightful moral and spiritual mentors of their children," Pastor David explained. "When Jesus established His Church, He did not say, 'Parents, relax! The Church will take care of your children from this point on.'

Mentoring children remains the responsibility of dads and moms."

Jason could not help but wonder how parents came to think that they could drop their kids off at the church doorstep and delegate the responsibility of developing their children into lovers of God.

Sarah raced through her memory banks, confirming that Julia's attitude and actions over the past year spelled out, in no uncertain terms, that her daughter talked, dressed, acted, walked and lived the same values as her unchurched friends.

As the implications of all this began to settle, both Jason and Sarah started to feel the weight of a terrible, irretrievable loss. The room seemed to shrink, almost robbing them of oxygen. Pastor David's office represented an inescapable, stark reality—their negligence had sealed Julia's fate. Her worldview was far from biblical, and it was now locked solidly into place. Only a major reconstruction—if that was even possible—could dislodge it.

Pastor David gently broke in on their thoughts. "Maybe it would be best if we discussed Julia's situation another time? I have a service coming up shortly, but please know that I'm here to help if there's anything I can do."

Jason and Sarah quickly rose to their feet. As they stood, Pastor David's instinct told him that their marriage was in trouble and that if this family was going to survive, he needed to tell them what they needed to do to find victory over their situation. *Don't let them go!* his instincts bellowed. *They have no clue what they're doing. They have no plan. They're trying to raise three children by the seats of their pants, and it isn't going to work. You've got to stop them!*

But as the fragile couple shook his hand and walked out into the harshness of the real world, a deeper, wiser voice answered gently from within Pastor David's heart: *Let them go. They have just started to listen. There is hope! God is able. He won't let their marriage sink. He won't let the children go without a fight.*

David picked up the Bible, still open to the passage in Proverbs. He straightened his tie, made a passing glance at his appearance in a small mirror and then headed for the church auditorium. Somewhere in the hallway, a terrifying thought stopped him in his tracks.

What a hypocrite! he thought to himself. *Who am I to offer spiritual direction to the Millstones?*

As the organist reached the closing notes of the prelude, David made a beeline to his wife, Catherine. "Honey, after the service we need to have a serious talk about our family," David intoned. Before Catherine could answer, he bounded to the platform and the service began. She remained perplexed until they were in the car and on their way home. That night, David and Catherine fell on their knees before God. They renewed a commitment to raise their children to know, love and serve the Lord Jesus Christ.

* * *

The drive home from church was a quiet one for the Millstones. Julia and Paige sat in the middle bucket seats of the family's tan minivan. They looked out their opposite windows and seemed lost in thought. Jeremy lay across the back seat with his inseparable GameBoy locked between his palms. He had not buckled his seatbelt and hoped his mother wouldn't notice.

Fortunately for Jeremy, his mother was distracted. She sat upright in the passenger seat—spine straight, shoulders back, hands neatly folded in her lap. Her eyes darted back and forth between the dashboard in front of her and the side mirror to her right. She chewed gently on her lower lip without realizing it.

Jason funneled all his effort and concentration into the act of driving. His hands grasped the wheel at ten and two and his eyes rotated from the road in front of him to the rearview mirror, over to the driver's side mirror and back to the road. He maintained his usual speed of exactly seven miles per hour over the speed limit. "Cops'll never bust a man for going seven over," he had confidently revealed to his family on several occasions.

The minivan rolled into the Millstone driveway and eased its way beneath the upraised garage door. The children spilled out one by one and wandered into the house. Jason and Sarah regarded each other in silence for another minute.

"I don't feel very encouraged," Sarah volunteered.

"Yeah," Jason agreed. "I see things better, but I have no idea where to begin."

"Why is it," Sarah asked, "that we don't go to school to become good parents?"

Jason laughed at the question. "Isn't that the truth! We have thirty years of education between the two of us, and for what? Our occupations?"

"Exactly!" Sarah chimed back in. "Just one year. That's all I ask . . . one measly year to learn how to train my children God's way."

Jason remained in his driver's seat as Sarah opened her car door and began to get out. "Are you coming in?" She asked.

"I need to run by the office," he said, holding out his hand like a crossing guard when his wife began to protest. "I just need to answer a few e-mails and print out some reports for my team meeting tomorrow morning. It'll only take an hour, max—I promise."

Sarah exhaled a long sigh of resignation. Jason reached over and caught her wrist as she began to pick up her purse and Bible from the seat. "I'll tell you what," he said, eyes sparkling, "why don't you call the babysitter while I'm gone, and let's go out tonight." Her eyes brightened noticeably and a smile tugged at the corners of her mouth.

"Where would we go?" she asked.

"Ozzy's!"

Sarah gasped and hopped back into the passenger seat like a toddler hopping onto Santa's lap. "Ozzy's!" she exclaimed. "But that's over an hour away."

Oswald's Lakefront Steakhouse nestled against the breathtaking scenery of the Lake of the Ozarks. The reputation of its prime rib and lobster bisque reached through several states. It was also the place where Jason and Sarah went on their very first date.

"I know," Jason answered, "but we could use something special tonight, don't you think?" Sarah did not answer with words, but leaned over and blessed the corner of her husband's mouth with a promising kiss. She hopped out of the car and bustled inside.

Jason entered his office ten minutes later and headed for the rolling leather chair behind his mahogany desk. Hopping in, he turned on his computer and typed in several successive passwords with practiced automation. Within seconds, the inbox of his private e-mail account materialized.

There were four new messages. The third was from A. Brownlow.

"Yes!" he shouted, hopping out of the chair to do a quick teenager-like spin. He plopped back into the chair, wheeled closer to the monitor, clicked his mouse on the name and began to read.

My Andrew,

I was very glad to get your letter. Things have been difficult at home recently—my husband and I seem to be struggling, you know—and I need your encouragement desperately.

Leaning back in his chair, Jason wondered what type of churlish scoundrel was married to his secret friend. He shook his head in disgust before continuing to read.

> But enough about all that. I'm so glad to hear that you
> are well! It makes my heart dance to hear that you're
> thinking of me . . . that you miss me. I can't think of
> anything else I'd rather hear.
>
> I'm not sure how many letters we have written to
> each other over the past few months (hundreds?) but I
> want you to know that I cherish each and every one.
> You have me dreaming again, Andrew. I dream of trop-
> ical lands waiting to be explored, of adventures to be
> experienced and someone to share them with who feels
> the same way I do about so many things.
>
> I have a question to ask you, Andrew, and I would
> very much like to hear you answer it the way I'm hop-
> ing you will answer it. Here goes . . . Would you like
> to meet? Face to face? I know this is a big step, but I
> think it could be wonderful. I haven't even let myself
> imagine what it would be like to have a conversation
> with you without this plastic keyboard and glass
> screen. To see your face . . . to hear your voice.

Jason tore his eyes away from the screen in front of him and
raised himself out of the chair, more slowly this time. He blinked
his eyes several times and rubbed his hands against his face.

What is happening here? he asked himself. *How did this inno-
cent dialogue with a phantom friend reach this place of serious emotional intensity?* Jason had no answer. Slowly the justifications
began to emerge. Sarah did not understand him anymore.
Their marriage had cooled. Romance had taken a permanent
leave. He desperately needed a listening ear. There was so
much more, but he had all he needed to turn his attention
back to Anita Brownlow.

He dashed back into the chair and devoured the rest of the letter.

What do you say, my Andrew? I will be having lunch on the boardwalk by the Lake of the Ozarks on Monday. Have you been there? I know a great place called Oswald's Lakeshore Steakhouse. If you want to make me happy, Andrew, please come and eat with me. Please come and talk with me. I'll be there at 12:30 and . . . I need you. Please say yes.

All my love,

Anita Brownlow

Jason blankly stared at the flickering screen. He reread the letter several times with his mouth slightly open. Every time his eyes reached the line, "I need you," his face split with the goofy grin of a high school sophomore holding hands with a girl for the first time.

Jason glanced at his watch and cursed softly. Hurriedly, he clicked his mouse over the button labeled "Reply." As he typed, Jason chose not to think about the odd coincidences that had surrounded his online relationship with Anita Brownlow. He didn't ponder the correlations between her life and his . . . between her husband's life and his own. He also did not think about the irony of her request to meet at Ozzy's.

As he finished his letter and sent it into the welcoming inbox of his secret love, he didn't think about his wife at all. He was taken by his passion for a dream woman who was everything he could ever hope for—and more.

CHAPTER 4

MELTDOWN

——

My Andrew,

I can't wait to see you! It makes me so happy just knowing that we'll be together soon . . . I can't even imagine what it will be like when I finally see you face to
face! 12:30 then, at Oswald's. I'll be carrying a red rose.

All my love,

Anita

Jason Millstone perched expectantly inside a padded, faux-
leather booth at Oswald's Lakeshore Steakhouse.

He was not an evil man. He was not a horrible person. He
was not even a terrible husband or father. He was merely the
glorious epitome of the American Dream before the blinders
fall off and everybody wakes up.

Jason had arrived at Ozzy's twenty minutes earlier. A waitress
deposited the third iced tea onto the table in front of him. His
heart was in his throat. Nervousness did not begin to describe
the tension in his soul. Jason was a driven man, but also a torn
man. His conscience was acting up now that cyber dreamland
was rapidly becoming all too real. Too late to run. His curiosity
refused to let him flee. He was in love with someone beyond

perfection. His mind would not permit dissent. Red flags were outlawed.

He had let his guard down and the enemy swept in with brutal force. Jason still knew right from wrong. The problem was his will. In allowing the enemy access to his heart, he inadvertently allowed himself to be bound and gagged. A hook pierced his nose. He no longer had anything to say about the matter. He found himself in complete bondage, helpless and powerless—and completely unaware of his plight.

He glanced at his watch. It was 12:37.

"No big deal," he muttered to reassure himself. "All classy women are fashionably late." He reminded himself that he can't refer to the restaurant as Ozzy's—that's what he and Sarah have always called it.

At the thought of his wife, a nagging voice began to buzz in the back of his mind.

For heaven's sake! it said, *you were here with your wife last night.*

The voice surprised and unsettled Jason. It seemed to emanate from thick, dark clouds forming in clumps over the horizon. It was time once again for a little self-justification. *Things have been difficult at home . . .*

From the back of his mind—something important, something that he needed to know, or figure out . . . *"I know a great place called Oswald's Lakeshore Steakhouse . . ."*

Quickly, Jason dismissed the pesky, flitting whisper. Whatever it wanted him to know could wait. He drowned it out with thoughts of all the wonderful aspects of his secret love. He thought of how humorous she had been in her e-mails, how her personality sparkled through the words.

He had to meet her. She wanted what he wanted in life. They were a perfect match. He thought of how thrilling she could be, how daring, how much she had practically *begged* to meet him here today!

Each endorphin-laced thought wrapped around his mind like a blanket. He gazed at the restaurant door—the pearly gates of his own, personal heaven. *Any minute now*, he thought, *those gates will swing open and usher in the most perfect woman ever to walk the face of this earth, my one and only, my secret love!*

As if reading his mind, the heavy door shuddered slightly and began to open. For Jason, the entire world condensed into one sweet inhalation—a single, frozen point of anticipation. He leaned forward expectantly, searching for love with a lovely red rose in hand.

After a slight pause to make one final adjustment to her hair, Sarah Millstone strolled confidently into the restaurant. She wore a deep-red, sleeveless blouse over a tight, knee-length skirt made of white linen. Her chin was upraised, her eyes sparkled. Several men waiting in the foyer stopped their conversation and discreetly watched as she walked by. Clutched tightly in her left hand was a long-stemmed rose the same color as her blouse.

Jason never saw that final clue. The moment Sarah came into view, his eyes locked in stunned panic on her face. Several seconds passed. A light gagging sound emerged from the back of his throat.

His mind finally threw off the tattered remains of the once-comforting blanket of anticipated bliss and slammed back into gear. He dove underneath the table—the same rectangular piece of wood that had, only seconds before, acted as the sacred altar of his passionate love.

His dive perfectly coincided with the re-arrival of the waitress carrying yet another glass of iced tea. The collision sent her sprawling to the floor with a surprised, frightened squawk. Sarah and the other patrons standing at the front of the restaurant turned to look at the sprawling form on the carpet, giving Jason a much-needed diversion.

Desperate, panting and bewildered, he scuttled on all fours across the aisle and down the ensuing row of booths. Panic took over. As Jason's muscles automatically flexed and relaxed in an effort to move away from the entrance as quickly as possible, he clipped the legs of another waitress—this one carrying a tray loaded with several bowls of lobster bisque—knocking her to the ground amid a deafening *crash*.

Jason didn't notice. He didn't hear the angry, bewildered cries of the other diners as they yelled for him to "Calm down, you idiot!" Crouching against the back of one of the larger booths, he looked around wildly.

To his right, a small, rectangular sign hung lazily against the wall facing away from the lake. Neon-orange block letters affirmed the situation and offered an escape—*Emergency Exit*.

With a strangled cry of determination and relief, Jason sprinted through a narrow aisle of chairs, leaped over a busboy picking up a bisque-less china bowl, and burst through the door. Once outside, he altered his trajectory slightly and continued his mad dash in the direction of his car, the ringing of the alarm from the activated emergency door fading behind him.

As he ran, his mind outraced him. One horrible thought pounded the center of his mind: *Fourteen years of marriage! Fourteen years of marriage! Fourteen years of marriage!* It drummed within his head, keeping pace with his feet like a horrible native chant, leaving him no opportunity to consider what Anita would think when she arrived at the restaurant and didn't find him there.

After Jason finally managed to release his keys from his pocket, he opened the door to the Honda Accord and collapsed behind the wheel—a shuddering heap of fear, confusion and gut-twisting dread. Still trying to make sense of what had happened, he took a deep breath and inserted the key into the ignition. Before starting the car, he took one last glance inside Ozzy's.

Looking through the half-shuttered windows, he saw his wife stoop to pull a lobster-bisque-drenched waitress to her feet. She was bent slightly at the knees and supported the waitress with her right hand.

She kept her left hand upraised and extended as if to keep it clear of the mess. The delicate, slender fingers of that hand were wrapped tightly around a single, red rose. Jason's thoughts, breath and heart stopped simultaneously.

Connections instantly formed, faded and reformed in Jason's brain. The weird similarities that he had ignored between Anita's life and his own—and between her husband's life and his own—came roaring into his thoughts. Like the metal tumblers of a combination lock, they clicked together in rapid succession, forcing him to recognize the harsh, unbearable truth.

Cold realizations—some long-suspected, some long-ignored—pierced his heart like arrows. *I've been cheating on my wife. My wife has been cheating on me. Anita is my wife. Sarah is my secret love. I had them both. I've lost them both. I've lost everything.*

Jason mechanically opened and closed his mouth as those painful facts were replaced by a streaming parade of images. Sarah on their wedding day . . . Julia as a newborn in the hospital . . . Paige losing her first tooth . . . Jeremy playing T-ball in a green uniform . . . the computer . . . the church . . . his hands . . .

Jason wheezed a low, despairing moan and turned the key.

* * *

Two hours later, Jason sat slumped at the end of a wooden pier. He had started to drive back to work after leaving the restaurant parking lot but changed his mind. Looking to his right, he could see the bustling activity at Ozzy's, now running as normal about a thousand feet away. *The scene of the crime*, he thought.

He shifted to look out over the placid lake before him.

Jason had never felt so alone.

He began to wonder for the hundredth time if his wife had seen him at the restaurant when a young voice to his left cried, "Pirates off the starboard bow!" Turning, Jason spied a blue-and-white paddleboat skimming slowly over the water about a hundred feet from the shore. Three boys were enjoying themselves—two peddling furiously in the front and the other crouched behind them. The crouching boy held a small plastic lever that controlled the rudder.

"No, Jimmy!" yelled one of the peddling boys, pointing toward Jason. "Starboard means 'right.' You're going the wrong way."

"Sorry!" Jimmy said, turning the lever in the opposite direction.

At first, Jason thought that he must be the "pirates" in question. Then a blurred motion caught the corner of his right eye. Swiveling toward it, he saw another paddleboat coming his way. This one also came outfitted with two young peddling boys and one younger captain behind them.

"Enemy sighted!" cried one of the peddlers from the boat on Jason's right. "Full speed ahead." The two boys in front begin peddling even faster, and the square-shaped craft lurched forward with a renewed burst of speed.

Jason watched, amused, as the two boats eventually thumped into each other with an anticlimactic *bonk*.

"We're hit, sir!" wailed Jimmy in despair from the back of boat number one.

"Grappling hooks secured," answered Bobby, grabbing hold of the second boat's plastic frame. "Prepare the boarding party!" In response, Jimmy stood up and rubbed his hands together excitedly.

"They're trying to board us!" cried one of the peddlers from boat number two.

"Reverse engines," his shipmate answered from behind him. Both boys in the front of the second boat began to pedal backward in an effort to retreat but wound up towing boat number one with them because of Bobby's tenacious grip.

Still standing upright in the back of boat number one, Jimmy stumbled and swayed as the two ships begin to move. Instinctively, the muscles in Jason's arms tightened and flexed. He pulled his dangling legs up, as if preparing to spring off the pier. Five years as a summer lifeguard and competitive swimmer created an automatic response.

Jimmy regained his balance and crouched down again behind the older boys in front of him. *Careful kid*, Jason thought.

"Send over the boarding party!" Bobby cried triumphantly, still holding on to the enemy vessel. In one fluid motion, Jimmy stood up again, stepped between the two peddlers in front of him, and leaped toward the front of the second boat.

Jimmy's left foot landed tenuously on the front edge of the other boat. In an attempt to steady himself, he tried to kick his right leg backward for solid footing on his own boat, but his wet, worn-out sneaker skidded on the blue plastic. The resulting slide buckled his left knee, and he fell forward.

With a sickening *crack* the side of Jimmy's head slammed into the front of boat number two. Jimmy's suddenly limp body rolled over the edge of both boats into the water and disappeared, fully clothed in tennis shoes, jeans and a sweatshirt. Horrified, the other boys stopped peddling, but their momentum continued to pull them away from their sinking friend.

In a flash, Jason dove into the water and swam toward them. The water was cool, but he hardly noticed. Several powerful strokes brought him to the place where he last saw the boy. Sucking in a huge gasp of air, he plunged downward.

Jason's body had adjusted to the temperature of the water, which was consistent for the first six feet. But beneath that, it quickly turned cold and dark. Even with his eyes wide open, he could only see two feet at best. Still propelling himself downward with furiously kicking legs, Jason extended his arms in front of him and waved them back and forth like a blind man grasping for his fallen cane.

After a few moments, his sweeping hand brushed a tangle of soft, stringy hair. He seized it and pulled the boy against him, slipping his left arm around Jimmy's chest.

Heart pounding, Jason kicked fiercely toward the surface. Once above the water, the cries of the other children, still floating numbly in their blue plastic squares, assaulted him.

"Dad! Dad! Help! Jimmy's hurt!"

Jason swam back to the pier and hoisted the child up a makeshift ladder tacked onto the end. Jason carefully laid the limp form on his stomach. He then pressed slowly and firmly on the boy's back. The child began to hack and sputter as a torrent of water flowed from his mouth.

Multiple footsteps pounded along the wooden planks, but Jason's attention was firmly focused on Jimmy. Jason sent up a prayer of thanks as the boy opened his eyes while continuing to spew lake water.

"Jimmy! Jimmy!" cried a panic-stricken middle-aged woman arriving as the boy attempted to sit up. Jason held his hand on the boy's chest and spoke gently.

"Son, lay flat for just a moment."

She got down on her knees to cradle the child, but Jason blocked her.

"Stay back," he said authoritatively, still gasping for breath. Then, after catching a glimpse of the woman's horrified face, he explained, "He hit his head pretty hard. We've got to be careful of his neck, just in case."

The woman turned pale, gulped and remained on her knees. Calmly, Jason asked the boy to wriggle his fingers. All ten moved.

Good. Then he asked the lad to wriggle his toes. No movement. *Not so good.* Jason turned to the others. "Let's find a blanket. He needs to be kept warm until the ambulance gets here."

Jason looked up at the group of people standing around him. "Has anyone called 911?"

A well-dressed man with a cell phone to his ear quickly responded. "Yes! They are on their way."

The man continued talking, and Jason could hear him telling the operator exactly where the pier was located. Nodding, Jason turned to the middle-aged woman still kneeling in front of him. He had little doubt this was the child's mother.

"I think he will be okay. Are you his mom?"

The woman could hardly speak. As tears welled in her eyes, she shook uncontrollably. "Thank you for saving my son!"

* * *

The paramedics had come and gone within a half hour. Little Jimmy had been a good soldier, remaining perfectly still—with the exception of his toes, which he had begun wriggling just before the ambulance pulled up, accompanied by the thunderous applause of his family and the growing crowd. Most of the crowd had dispersed by the time the paramedics had Jimmy strapped on the stretcher and on his way to the hospital.

A kind lady who had brought blankets from her boat and the man who had called 911 were carrying on a dialogue about unsupervised kids and docks. The other children from the paddleboats milled around anxiously on the beach behind them. Several times assurances were given that they were not in trouble, but the boys remained unsure.

Jason sat on a wooden bench near the front of the pier. He helped a congenial police officer complete an incident report.

When they were finished, the officer shook Jason's hand, clapped him on the shoulder and left.

Jason beamed. *What a day!* he thought. *In fact, this day will never be forgotten.* Then reality dashed in, stealing every ounce of euphoria. He needed to go home. His clothing was still wet. *Home? Sarah? Oh, Lord! What have I done?* He got up slowly, and with measured footsteps began to shuffle in the direction of his car.

"Thank God you were here today!" the Blanket Lady blurted out. "I don't know what we would have done if anything worse had happened."

Jason turned to see that Blanket Lady and Cell Phone Man had caught up with him. Suddenly the woman enveloped Jason in a grateful bear hug.

She howled ecstatically, "You, sir, are a wonderful man!"

Jason blushed. "It was my pleasure," he wheezed when she finally let him go.

Immediately, the man with the cell phone seized Jason's hand. "Lionel Johnson," he said, grinning widely, "and this is my wife, Angela." *Blanket Lady and Cell Phone Man are husband and wife.*

"Jason Millstone," Jason answered, feeling a bit awkward. Both of them stared at him with unabashed gratefulness and awe. "Do you know little Jimmy?"

"Actually, yes," Angela answered, as another small wave of anxiety washed over her features. "Our families live in the same Midland neighborhood. Jimmy's parents have a boat in the marina and he and his mom and brother, Bobby, come here often in the summer to hang out until their dad joins them after work."

"It's not going to be any fun bringing Bobby home without his brother," Lionel said, rubbing the back of his neck nervously. "But thank God you were here, or Jimmy might not have come home at all."

"It was nothing." Jason thought to throw some humor into the conversation. "I used to be a lifeguard and I needed some practice."

Lionel smiled broadly. "Your timing, not to mention your stroke, was picture perfect."

The Johnsons' repeated offerings of "Thank God you were here" reminded Jason exactly why he *was* here, and the scorching memory of Sarah walking through the restaurant door flashed across his mind. Guilt and shame settled back into his gut like lead weights. Then an impossibly bizarre thought freight-trained into his brain. *God was in this. He allowed me to see clearly the foolishness of my selfish ways back at Ozzy's, and then he sat me down on a dock at the right time and the right place.*

"Here's my info," Lionel said, handing Jason a white business card. "If you ever need a hand with *anything*, just give me a call, okay?"

"Sure," Jason mumbled, glancing down at the card before stuffing it into his front pocket. He didn't feel like talking anymore and began to back away from the still-smiling couple.

"Have a nice day." Hand clutching his stomach, Jason turned away and began swishing his wet pant legs toward the parking lot.

"Thanks, mister!" a young voice called out from the beach. Jason assumed it must belong to Jimmy's brother, Bobby. He waved to the boys and disappeared between several SUVs.

The images were coming faster now—Sarah, the rose, the waitress—flitting in and out of his mind like accusatory birds. Beginning to weep all over again, he drove past Oswald's Lakeshore Steakhouse one last time before heading back to Midland.

* * *

Once at home, Jason stood in the garage for several minutes before he could bring himself to step through the door and face his wife. He took a deep breath, attached a fake smile to his face and threw open the door.

Everything seemed strangely normal. The wedding pictures still hung on the wall in front of the stairs. That was a positive sign. He had already taken note that none of his clothes or books were strewn across the front lawn. The unmistakable fragrance of baking lasagna added further intrigue to the gut-wrenching moment.

Beginning to feel hopeful, Jason walked into the living room. Jeremy and Paige were at their usual stations. Jeremy was slumped in Jason's chair with his eyes glued to his GameBoy, and Paige was perched in front of the computer.

"Hi, kids," Jason said, trying to sound cheerful.

"Hi, Dad," the children said in unison without turning around.

"Uh . . . have either of you seen your mother?" To Jason's surprise, both of the children swiveled to look at him, their faces sober. Tasting bile in the back of his throat, Jason held his breath.

Paige answered, "She went to the store to pick up something she needed for dinner."

Jason exhaled slowly, then thought, *Geez, I was in the garage for ten minutes and I didn't even notice that her car wasn't there.* "Idiot," he muttered under his breath.

He started to ask another question, but Paige cut him off by saying, "She was crying when she left."

"Oh, really?" Jason asked, trying to look surprised and concerned. He leaned nonchalantly against the back of the couch before asking, "Did she say why she was upset?"

Jeremy and Paige both shook their heads.

"Huh," Jason grunted. "Well, I'm sure she's okay. We'll make sure to give her a big hug when she comes back, okay?" The children readily agreed, then returned to their previous activities.

If she comes back, Jason thought, sighing heavily. Still leaning against the back of the couch, he watched his daughter's fingers dance lightly across the keyboard. *That's the keyboard that Anita uses*, he realized. He started to flop back onto the couch when a frightening thought occurred to him.

Catching himself, he asked, a bit too loudly, "Who are you writing to, Paige?"

"Just some friends, Dad," she answered.

"Which friends?" he pressed, and this time Paige heard a strange crack in her father's voice. She looked up.

"It's Molly and Rachel, from my soccer team." She held his eyes for a moment before glancing back at the screen and pointing. "See?"

Jason stood behind her and peered down at the screen. Three screen names were present in what looked to be a private, online chat room. The first, *Turn_the_Paige*, belonged to his daughter. He had helped her think of that one last year. The other two were *Goalie_Girl123* and *Molly.Simmons*.

"How do I know that's really Rachel?" he asked.

"Dad!" Paige cried in exasperation.

"All right, all right," Jason conceded. He squeezed her shoulder gently before walking back to the front of the couch. Feeling exhausted, he turned on the TV.

His own picture stared back at him from the top-right corner of the screen.

" . . . dramatic rescue on the Lake of the Ozarks today," the anchorman intoned. "James Chambers—the youngest son of Jake Chambers, mayor of Midland—sustained a severe concussion after hitting his head on the side of a rented watercraft earlier this afternoon . . ."

"The mayor's son?" Jason whispered, not believing what he had just heard.

"Witnesses said the boy was rescued by a local man present at the scene of the accident."

"Dad, that's you!" Jeremy cried, dropping his GameBoy into his lap and pointing at the TV screen. Stunned, Jason sat up on the couch and watched as the news report cycled through almost a dozen photographs of the pier, the crowd of people, and the paramedics loading Jimmy into the ambulance. The last three pictures showed Jason, wrapped in a large towel, talking with a police officer.

"You saved someone's life?" Paige squeaked from behind him.

"I . . ." Jason began, but was unable to speak. Thinking back, he remembered the oily-looking man with the camera who had been taking pictures. Jason hadn't given him a second thought at the time.

"Shh!" Jeremy hissed when Paige again asked for an explanation. "Listen to the story!"

" . . . dove into the murky waters and pulled the boy to safety," the anchorman said. "Mr. Millstone is a resident of Midland and currently works as a sales representative for Van Hutchinson's Investments." Turning to a younger woman sitting next to him, the anchorman added, "It's always nice to feature a local hero, don't you think?"

"It sure is," she answered, "and that's a remarkable, heartwarming story." Pause. "In national news, the president is preparing for his summit in Switzerland this weekend . . ."

Feeling numb, Jason turned off the television.

"Is it true, Dad? Is it true?" burst Paige, now sitting next to him on the couch.

"Yeah, it's true," Jason admitted, rubbing the back of his neck. Sparing a few gory details, he told them the story. Both children listened with rapt attention and gazed up at their father with worshiping eyes. Watching them made him feel very dirty.

"I'm proud of you, Dad," Paige said when the story was over. She slid over and hugged her father's side, but jumped back immediately. "Whoa, you're still wet!"

"Really?" Jason said in an unbelieving tone of voice. A quick check confirmed that dampness remained. "I guess I didn't notice."

"Mom's not going to be happy about you being on the couch when she gets home," Jeremy chided. He could authenticate his assertion through past experience.

All three turned at the sound of the front door opening. The fuzzy-plastic rustle of grocery bags rubbing together was followed by the inside door to the garage slamming shut. Jason gulped and stood up, trying to figure out what kind of face he should wear. Sarah walked into the living room.

She was still wearing the skirt and blouse from earlier and still looked like a million bucks. But her confident stride and upraised chin were gone, replaced with a heaviness and red, bleary eyes. It was obvious—even to Jason—that she had been crying. A lot.

"Mom, Dad rescued a boy my age today!" Jeremy called out while running over to her.

"Yeah," echoed Paige, reaching her first, "he saved him from drowning!"

"What?" Sarah asked, looking bewilderedly at her husband. "What kind of game are you playing?"

"It's true, Mom," Jeremy called, tugging on her sleeve. "We saw it on the news!"

"Yeah, yeah," Paige continued. "A kid fell out of his boat on the Lake of the Ozarks, and Dad dove in and saved him!"

At the mention of the lake, the color vanished from Sarah's face. A bag full of grapes and honeydew slipped from her fingers and landed on the living room floor with a wet *thud*. Sarah didn't notice.

"Wha . . . ?" She began, forcing herself against the wall to steady herself before she could speak. She looked at Jason with eyes full of fear and pain. "What were you doing by the Lake of the Ozarks today?"

Jason's mind burst into action, offering and discarding possible scenarios at lightning speed. A second of awkward silence passed. "I . . . uh, I left my cell phone at Ozzy's last night and had to go back for it."

Interesting, Jason thought to himself. *One sin gives birth to another sin.*

"Oh," Sarah answered, still leaning precariously against the wall. Then, acting as if it were the least important question in the world, she asked, "What time did you get there?"

"Umm, about two o'clock."

"Oh," Sarah said again, still trying to appear indifferent. But her face betrayed her. Jason saw a wave of relief sweep across it. In another second, a similar wave washed over his own face.

Everything's going to be okay, now, he told himself, almost believing it—but not quite. Somewhere in the back of his mind he heard the words, "Your sin will find you out."

Letting go of the wall, Sarah knelt and deposited the rest of the grocery bags onto the floor. "Kids," she said, looking down at Jeremy and Paige, "could you please put these away in the kitchen?" Something in her voice and eyes prompted them to obey without a word. As soon as they were gone, she slumped back against the wall and looked up at Jason.

"I'm really not feeling very well tonight," she said, awkwardly jerking her hand toward her midsection. "Something's weird with my stomach. I have lasagna in the oven and the timer is set. Could you take care of dinner?"

"Be happy to, dear."

"Good," said Sarah, beginning to slide away from the wall. "I think I'm going to lie down for a while." When she reached the entrance to the hall, she turned back to her husband and asked, "Were you really on the news?" Jason nodded, unable to speak in the face of his wife's emotional struggle. "Set the TiVo to record the late news . . . see if you can catch something I can watch tomorrow." And then she was gone.

After presiding over dinner, making sure Jeremy and Paige brushed their teeth and forcing Julia to promise that she would remain in her room for the rest of the night, Jason slipped into bed beside his wife and fell into a restless sleep.

He woke up a few hours later, alone. Looking at the illuminated clock resting on his bedside table, Jason saw that it was almost one o'clock in the morning. Feeling sick, he slipped out of bed and walked quietly to the top of the stairs.

Below, the wall to the left of the kitchen was highlighted by a soft, blue light. *She's Anita, now*, Jason thought, gripping the railing at the top of the stairs. *She's writing to find out why I didn't show up.*

Straining his ears, Jason could make out the faint *click-tick-tack* of his wife using the family keyboard to type secret messages to another man. The sound distressed him.

Soon another sound echoed through the hall and up the carpeted staircase, a sound that locked Jason's heart inside a merciless vice: the sound of a desperate woman weeping softly and asking, "Why, Andrew? Why?"

Backing away from the awful sounds and the accusing blue light, Jason eased himself back into bed and spent the rest of the night pretending to sleep. Slowly it became clear to him: The sovereign God Jason worshiped would not let this drama vanish quietly into the night. The handwriting was on the wall. Jason and Sarah had been measured and found standing naked in their own sins. The Lord of heaven and Earth would surely act. But how? When? Jason had no answers, only a sense of dread.

CHAPTER 5

FAME

———

Jason couldn't decide which emotion was worse as he dragged through the front door of Van Hutchinson's Investments: loneliness or shame. Or maybe it was the deep fatigue that dogged his every step. *Could this be the true weight of sin?* He thought to himself. If the strain showed, Jason's coworkers did not acknowledge it.

"Hey, Jason!" called a round little man from the elevator. "Saw you on the news last night, champ. Way to go!"

"Thanks, Charlie," Jason mumbled, glancing down into the man's eager, sweaty face. He tried to muster a smile.

"Wow!" Charlie continued, "The mayor's son. Man! You gotta tell me all about it!"

Sighing, Jason reached for the elevator button, but then thought better of it. "You going up?" he asked.

"Sure am!" Charlie replied, flashing Jason a double thumbs-up at the same time.

"Uh-huh." Jason returned the gesture with only one hand. "I think I feel like the stairs today. Need the exercise." Without waiting for a response, he turned on his heel and plunged through a metal doorway to the right of the elevator.

A tall man with large glasses and an even larger smile intercepted Jason as he emerged from the staircase on the fourth floor. "Mr. Millstone!" he chirped, sliding in front of his target. "It's a pleasure to speak with you, sir."

"Uh, right," Jason spluttered, watching his hand become engulfed between the slender fingers of his assailant. "Listen, I'm a little la . . ."

"I would like to congratulate you, my dear Mr. Millstone," the tall man interrupted, "on your gallant rescue yesterday afternoon. Truly inspiring."

He shook Jason's hand as he spoke, his grin widening with each pump. "If you have a moment, sir, I would like to inquire about the . . ."

"Sorry, can't right now," Jason barked, yanking his hand away from his oppressor's still-pumping fists. "I'm running late for a conference call," Jason explained, somewhat apologetically. He backed away from the man with quick, furtive hops.

As he turned around, Jason collided with what felt like a bulldozer and careened against the wall. Dazed, Jason looked up and found himself staring directly into the swollen face of Travis Ellison. A member of Jason's sales team, Travis defined "mountain of a man." He stood as tall as Jason but tipped the scale at three hundred and twenty pounds. A round chin jutted from beneath a cavernous mouth. His dark brown hair was cropped with military precision and a small, round nose looked as if it had landed in the middle of his face after being hurled from another state.

"Hey, buddy, why don't you watch where you're . . ." Travis started in his gravelly voice, but he stopped when he saw his now-famous coworker, his eyebrows rising together in happy recognition. "Jason!" he gasped. "Hey, I want to hear all about . . ."

But Jason interrupted him, "Hi, Travis. It is a cool story, but I'll have to tell you about it later," Jason stammered. "Sorry, man, I have a conference call with a very important client and I'm running late, so I'll talk to you at lunch. See you then."

As the words spewed from Jason's mouth, he drew his cell phone from its clip like a gunslinger at high noon and held it in the air. He backed down the hall until he could duck through the narrow door leading into his department. Once inside, he slumped against the wall next to his office door.

"Good morning, Mr. Millstone," said a high, cheerful voice from behind him. Turning, Jason saw Marlene, the department secretary, looking up at him from her seat. Her bright blue eyes sparkled under a mass of shiny blond hair, her pointed chin perched lightly on her hands.

"Marlene," Jason said, languidly returning his cell phone to his belt. "I don't want any interruptions this morning, okay? No visitors, no phone calls . . . nothing."

Marlene cleared her throat as Jason reached for the doorknob. He turned. "Is something wrong?" she asked, throwing worried glances toward Jason's office door. "It's just that . . . you already have a visitor."

Jason sighed. "In my office?" he asked. She nodded. "Fine," Jason said. "I'll take care of this person. Just don't let anyone else in. Understand?"

"Oh, Mr. Millstone," Marlene spluttered, throwing another anxious look at the office door. "It's just that . . ."

"No questions, Marlene," Jason cut in, raising his left hand and bringing it back down in a chopping motion. "I have an important matter I am dealing with and I just need some space." Without another word, Jason opened the door and stepped inside.

A middle-aged man, wearing an expensive Italian suit stood behind Jason's desk, peering out the fourth floor window onto the busy street below. The figure was tall with broad shoulders, his long, solid arms crossed behind his back. Dark hair was slicked against his skull. *Just like Pat Riley,* Jason thought.

"I appreciate you coming this morning," Jason said, gruffly, dropping his briefcase. "But I don't have time for any presentations."

The intruder turned at the sound of his voice, and Jason stepped back in surprise. There was something vaguely familiar about the man—something about his brown eyes, sharp nose and salt-and-pepper goatee that Jason couldn't quite put a finger on. Smiling broadly, the man strode briskly across the room with both of his arms raised as if inviting an embrace.

"Jason, my man," he said in a low, smooth voice. "I'm terribly sorry to intrude, but I just had to thank you in person. My wife would never forgive me otherwise, you know." He clasped Jason's right hand and shoulder, squeezing them both while flashing another wide, knowing smile. "Jake Chambers," Midland's mayor said, squeezing Jason's shoulder one more time before letting go. "Do you think you could spare me a minute or two?"

"Oh . . . of course, Your Honor," Jason breathed, embarrassed about his brusque attitude only a moment ago.

"No, no," the mayor of Midland returned, wagging a long finger back and forth in front of his face. "Any man who saves my son's life is going to call me Jake, got that?"

"Okay," Jason answered. "Would you like to sit down?"

The mayor walked with Jason across the room to two small leather chairs.

"I'm honored that you would come all this way," Jason said, smiling. "How is Jimmy doing today?"

"He's doing great! If you saw him right now, you wouldn't think anything bad had happened yesterday."

Jason flashed another smile, revealing his genuine pleasure at hearing this.

"Mayor Chambers, if there is anything I can do for you or little Jimmy . . ."

"Well, there is! But first and foremost," the mayor responded, reaching across the desk and shaking Jason's hand once again, "I really do want to thank you. You saved my boy's life, and I don't think there's any way I could ever repay you."

The sincerity of the man's voice caused Jason to blush, but he resisted the urge to look away. Instead, he held the mayor's gaze and said, "Thank you, sir. I'm just glad I could help." Then he added, "Have the doctors given Jimmy a clean bill of health?"

"Yes, thank God," the mayor answered, nodding his head. "They kept him in the hospital overnight just to make sure, but his doctor is confident there was no . . . permanent . . . damage . . ." hesitating, he pointed to his head. Jason nodded his understanding and noticed that his guest was blinking back tears. This time he looked away.

A few moments later, the mayor continued. "Anyway, there is another reason I came down here today." Intrigued, Jason looked up. "I had a meeting with the governor last week. Apparently, the powers-that-be are interested in rebuilding our nation's civic pride."

"Which powers?" Jason asked.

"Well, the president, to begin with," answered the mayor, smiling at Jason's surprised look. "Yes, the president of the United States plans to launch a media campaign, and an integral part of his plan is to identify role models and publicly recognize them. The public relations blitz will move from them to other people who keep this country running on all cylinders—the everyday Americans who take on the dirty jobs that make this country the greatest in the world. Get the drift?"

Jason wasn't sure where this was going but nodded for the mayor to continue.

"Well, last week the governor asked me to keep an eye open for exceptional people, people who are willing to serve as an inspiration to the rest of us." The mayor paused for a moment, looking directly at Jason, and added, "People like you."

"Me?" Jason asked. "I don't know, Your Honor, I'm just a . . ."

"No," the mayor cut in, once again wagging his long finger in front of his face. "I told you before, it's Jake."

"Okay, Jake," Jason said. "It's just that . . ."

"I'm afraid I'm not going to take no for an answer," the mayor declared, smiling brightly. "I have no idea how you came to be on that pier yesterday, but I'm convinced that there are bigger things going on here than you, me and my boy. Are you a religious man, Jason?"

"Uh, yes . . . I'm a Christian," Jason answered, although his voice had become soft and choked. Seeing the mayor of Midland in his office had provided a temporary reprieve from the guilt, shame and fear that had taken residence in his mind since he saw the red rose in Sarah's hand the day before. Now it came flooding back.

"Good, good," the mayor continued. "I am, too. And I think the hand of Providence is at play here. I think you were divinely appointed to save my son's life, and I mean to do anything I can to show my gratitude to you and to the good Lord Himself."

Jason didn't answer. *Divinely appointed*, he thought. *That is true. But, I'm also an adulterer at heart, and I have defrauded my family.*

Taking Jason's silence as a sign of acceptance, the mayor reached into his pocket and pulled out a flat, rectangular box. After opening it, he turned it around for Jason to see. A golden medallion with the word "hero" etched across its face sparkled brilliantly from the box.

"Mr. Jason Millstone," intoned the mayor. Jason looked up at the sound of his name. "It is my privilege to appoint you the very first Hero of Midland."

Jason was dumbfounded. "Hero?" he asked. The word was incompatible with the tide of hopelessness currently washing in and out of his mind.

"That's right," the mayor answered. "I'm pretty sure you're the first person in the country to receive this award, since I only learned of this program last week. I even got our local engraver up an hour early this morning to inscribe your name."

As he spoke, the mayor lifted out the medallion and stood. With the broadest smile of the morning, he placed the lanyard portion over Jason's head and neck. The attached medallion came to a rest in the middle of his chest.

Stepping back, the mayor took a long, appraising look. "It's a natural fit," he said, beaming. Jason couldn't help but get caught up in the mayor's enthusiasm. He started to lighten up and enjoy the moment.

The mayor gasped, looking down at his watch. "I'm a little late for a meeting with some of the aldermen. But before I go . . ." He reached into his breast pocket and pulled out a business card. "This is my personal card, for friends only," he said, handing it to Jason. "It has my cell phone number and direct office extension. If you ever need anything, you just give me a call, okay? Oh, and by the way, Jason, the media will be all over this shortly. I noticed in the news yesterday how photogenic you are. Keep smiling! America needs some real heroes, and you are definitely one of them."

The mayor gave Jason's shoulder one final squeeze before walking briskly toward the door. He stopped and turned. "My executive assistant will be sending out a press release as soon as I get back to the office. I plan to hang that medal around your neck in the public square real soon. America will be there. Buckle up . . . it's going to be an exciting ride!" With a final wink and a wave of his hand, the mayor stepped through the office door, leaving Jason alone to drown in an ever-rising sea of self-loathing.

"That's awesome!" Travis Ellison roared a few hours later. He sat at a small table in a corner of the company lunchroom with Jason, who had just finished telling him about the events of the previous day and his morning meeting with Mayor Chambers. The big man reached out and slapped Jason on the shoulder. "Where's the medal, man?"

"In my desk drawer."

"Well," Travis grunted, "you're gonna have to pull it out for me as soon as we get back." He tore a large bite out of a mountainous roast beef sandwich, eyes growing wide. "Hey," he said, chewing vigorously with his mouth open, "we gotta tell Carl about this!" The words were muffled amid roast beef, provolone cheese and rye bread.

"No," Jason said. "I'm not telling Carl and neither are you."

Travis swallowed painfully before protesting, "Aw, come on, man! It'll make him so jealous he won't be able to stand it."

Jason shook his head. "Uh-uh, Travis." He dropped his voice. "I don't really want this getting around the company if I can help it."

"What?" Travis asked, looking puzzled. "But this is the coolest thing that's happened to you since I've known you."

Jason sighed deeply before responding. "I don't know, man. I just don't feel like I deserve all this attention, you know? I'm not a hero."

"Are you kidding?" Travis cried. "You saved that kid's life!"

"I did that," Jason answered. He picked up his own sandwich, held it distastefully in front of his chin for a few moments and then put it back down. "But there are hundreds of lifeguards who do the same thing every summer. Not to mention cops and firemen. Why should I get all this credit when they risk their lives every day?"

Travis threw a barrel-sized thermos jug to his lips before answering. "It's apples and oranges, man. Those people all get paid to do that stuff. It's their job. You," he pointed a salami-sized finger at Jason for emphasis, "you jumped in after that kid because you're a stand-up guy, and you deserve anything that comes your way because of it."

"Yeah," Jason breathed, nodding his head slowly. "I deserve what's coming to me." He looked down at his uneaten food.

A cold ball of guilty concrete stuffed his stomach.

"Hey," Travis asked, "What were you doing over at those docks yesterday anyway?"

"I'm sorry?" Jason muttered, stuffing his lunch back into a brown paper bag.

"The lake? Why were you there instead of here? Were you meeting a client out there or something?"

"Yeah," Jason grunted, pressing his hand to his gut. "Something like that. Listen, man, I'm not too hungry right now. I think I'm going to get back to work."

Travis started to protest as Jason reached into the paper bag and pulled out a Twinkie. "Think you could take care of this for me?"

Travis's eyes grew wide with anticipation. "I knew you were a hero, man," he said, snatching up the pastry and tearing into its shrink-wrapped shell with thick fingers. "This is the food of champions!"

"I'll see you back upstairs," Jason said, smiling grimly in spite of himself.

After easing into his office chair, Jason stared intently for several moments at a small drawer on the right side of his desk. With a sigh, he reached over and pulled it open. His left hand moved forward, gliding slowly toward the flat, rectangular box— then stopped. "No," Jason said, slamming the drawer shut with enough force to knock over a cup filled with pens above it. As he reached over to collect the pens, he noticed a red light flashing on the bottom-right corner of his phone. He picked up the receiver and pressed the small button labeled "Voicemail," then punched in the four digits of his password.

"You have three new messages," a voice chirped into his ear. "To listen to your messages, press One now."

"Hello, Mr. Millstone. This is Deborah Ammons. I'm a producer for Channel Five Action News. We received a press release from the mayor's office concerning your recent appointment as the first 'Hero of Midland.' I'd like to extend heartfelt congratulations on behalf of myself and all of us here at Channel 5. I would also like to talk to you about a possible interview this evening. We're running a feature on your status as the city's first hero, and we'd like to send a film crew to your office . . ."

Jason pressed a button. "Message skipped," the phone chirped cheerfully. "Next message."

"Mr. Millstone. Tyler Monroe from Channel Seven Nightly News. Let me be the first to congratulate you on your recent appointment as 'Hero of Midland.' That's quite an honor, sir. To show our appreciation for all you've done, we've put together a small dinner here at the station in your honor. If you could stop by around five o'clock, we'd love to . . ."

"Message skipped. Next message."

"Mr. Millstone! Skyler Thompson from Channel 32. I would just like to say . . ."

"Message skipped. End of messages . . ."

"Holy smokes," Jason whispered, hanging up the phone like a man waking up from a dream. Less than a second later, it erupted into a wild bray of electric noise. Startled, Jason scooted backward in his rolling leather chair. The phone rang a second time. Jason tentatively picked it up.

"Van Hutchinson's Investments, Jason Millstone speaking."

"Good afternoon, Mr. Millstone," a female voice answered. "My name is Cynthia Perez, from the Channel 2 Evening News."

"Hello, Cynthia," Jason cut in. "Listen, I appreciate the call, but I'm just not able to stop by your station this evening. I've got a prior commitment at home, you know."

"I thought you might be busy this evening, Mr. Millstone," she answered, sounding a little amused. "That's why I decided to come see you instead."

"See me?" Jason mumbled, feeling a little foolish but unable to do anything about it. "Me?"

"That's right, Mr. Millstone. I'm in the lobby of your office building right now. Do you think I could take just five minutes of your time before you head home to the family?"

Oh man, Jason thought, looking out his window and spotting a large, white van emblazoned with the words "Channel 2 News at 9." *What have I gotten myself into?*

"Mr. Millstone?" Cynthia said, "Are you still there?"

"Yes, ma'am," Jason answered, opening a small drawer on the right side of his desk. He pulled out the flat, rectangular box. "I'm still here."

* * *

The shadows deepened along the flower-lined path leading to the Millstone's front door. The savory smell of briquettes and BBQ marinade wafted across the threshold of his home as Jason pulled open the storm door. He let it slam behind him to announce his arrival.

"Dad's home," Jeremy announced from the kitchen. Sarah was the only one to greet him in the hallway.

"Hi, honey," she said, looking and sounding much improved from the night before. "Did the people at work see you on the news last night?"

"Oh, some of them mentioned they had caught a glimpse, yes," Jason answered, smiling again in spite of himself.

"Well you'll never believe what's been happening here," she said, tossing her hair mischievously.

"Let me guess," Jason replied, "A bunch of news stations have been calling to see if I can come down to their building and do an interview."

"Oh, yes," Sarah said, waving a dismissive hand in front of her face. "There were some of those. But that's not what I'm talking about."

"What then?" Jason asked, feeling genuine curiosity now.

"They came here!" Sarah cried, moving toward him and clasping his hands. "Channel Two came here to interview *us*."

"Us?" Jason stammered, half-laughing at the sight of his wife jumping up and down in front of him like a toddler trying to keep an exciting secret.

"Me and the kids. They wanted to get our thoughts on your dramatic rescue yesterday!"

"Wow," Jason breathed, feeling a healthy respect for the tenacity of the Channel 2 News Team. "What did you tell them?"

"Ah, ah, ah," Sarah scolded, wagging her finger in front of him. "You'll just have to wait until nine o'clock and see for yourself. But until then," she touched the tip of his nose with her index finger, "we've got chicken on the grill and mashed potatoes warming in the oven. Your favorite. Come on in and say hi to the kids, okay?"

"I'll be right there," Jason answered, "just let me put away my things." Watching his wife walk back into the kitchen, two powerful thoughts hammered Jason's consciousness. *What are you so happy about all of a sudden?* and *When did you start looking so good?*

Just as the morning visit from the mayor temporarily suspended his guilt and shame, the pleasant evening meal momentarily drove away the darkening clouds of unworthiness that had piled over his mind since he first saw the mocking word of judgment etched across the gold medallion. Sarah and Paige chattered about the visit from the news crew like two happy sparrows fluttering in and out of a nest. Jeremy looked up from a mountain of potatoes occasionally to correct a detail in the story. Even Julia piped in with comments and opinions. That night, the Millstone family operated as a well-tuned piece of machinery—no fights, no complaints, no extended periods of awkward silence.

Jason listened like a man who truly understood the miracle of a functioning family. To his relief, Sarah, Paige, Jeremy and

Julia were content to do all of the talking. No one asked him to "Tell us the story again, please!" No one demanded to see his shiny new medal. No one wondered aloud why he was sitting at the end of a pier along the Lake of the Ozarks when he should have been at work.

But the reprieve was merely temporary. After the dessert of angel food cake had been served and the dishes cleared and washed, a cruel window reopened in Jason's mind, allowing the black, pulsing clouds to resume their incessant march toward the center of his heart. *You're a fraud,* the clouds rumbled in shame-filled thunder. *An adulterous, fame-hungry fraud.*

After what seemed to Jason like the briefest of moments, the family assembled in the living room to watch the nine o'clock news.

"Hurry up, Mom!" Paige squealed as she and Jeremy plopped on either side of Jason on the couch. "It's starting!"

"Sorry," Sarah said, breathlessly, a minute later. "I just wanted to make sure your grandma was watching." She eased into the black and white recliner next to her youngest daughter while Julia slumped into the seat closest to Jeremy. In the middle of them all, Jason held his hand against his stomach and took a long, shuddering breath.

"Nervous, honey?" Sarah asked, affectionately patting his leg.

"I'm sweating bullets!" he answered, trying hard not to sound quite as wretched as he felt. Looking into his wife's sparkling, child-like eyes, he was again struck by how much she had changed from the night before. *How can you be so happy right now?* he wondered, trying to avoid the bitterness tucked away in the cramped crevices of that question.

Jeremy turned up the volume on the TV as the Channel Two logo scrolled across the screen. Like the night before, Jason's picture popped into view.

"Good evening," the well-groomed female anchor began. "Our top story tonight continues the saga of a local man's daring rescue of the mayor's son. As a result of that heroic action, Channel Two has learned that Jason Millstone is the first person in the country to receive a very special award. Cynthia Perez has the story."

The scene shifted to the wooden pier extending into the Lake of the Ozarks. A young Latino woman stood close to the spot where Jason had sat only a day before. He recognized her from their interview earlier in the day.

"Thank you, Joan. It all started yesterday on this very pier, when nine-year-old James Chambers slipped and fell out of a rented paddleboat. The young boy suffered a concussion when his head struck the side of the boat, causing him to sink quickly into the murky waters of the lake . . ."

Jason listened with intensifying dread as the reporter described his rescue efforts. Words like "courageous," "brave" and "daring" burned through his ears like furious, fiery bees.

The camera zoomed in on Cynthia Perez as she said, "I spoke with Mr. Millstone earlier this afternoon in the lobby of Van Hutchinson's Investments, Inc."

A quick burst of darkness filled the room as the TV screen flashed away from the lakeside pier, reemerging just inside the main doors of Jason's workplace. The rest of his family squealed with delight as the camera filmed Jason leaving the elevator and walking slowly, hesitantly, toward Ms. Perez. With another lightless flash, Jason's chest, shoulders, and head appeared in the middle of the screen.

"I guess I'm having a hard time understanding all the attention," television-Jason said flatly. "I mean, I think most people would do anything they could to help a child in danger. I was just in the right place at the right time to make a difference, that's all."

Unable to watch himself on the screen, Jason looked down at his son. The boy stared intently at the TV with an expression of undiluted awe. Inside Jason's mind, the thunderheads rumbled and churned. *Fraud. Fraud. Fraud.* A brilliant spike of hot, guilt-charged lightning streaked behind his eyes, making him wince.

"When I walked into my office and saw the mayor, I just had no clue what was going on," television-Jason continued. "When he gave me the award," the camera zoomed in briefly to capture the shining gold medallion dangling from his neck, "I don't know . . . I think I felt more than anything that I didn't really deserve it." The screen flashed once again, returning to Cynthia Perez at the Lake of the Ozarks.

"Mr. Millstone is referring to a visit he received earlier this morning from Mayor Jake Chambers, who officially appointed him the first Hero of Midland." Mayor Chambers himself quickly replaced Perez on the screen.

"It's a great honor to present Jason with such an award," he said. "Cities across the country will be nominating their own heroes in the coming year, but I'm excited to announce that Jason is the first person in the entire nation to receive the award. But more than that, I'm just thrilled to be able to recognize someone who . . ." the mayor's voice trailed off as he fought back tears for the second time that day. "I'm real happy to recognize someone who saved my son's life. I'm glad he was there to rescue my boy, and I'm glad to have him as an honored citizen of our town. Jason Millstone is certainly my hero!"

Holding back tears, Sarah reached over and squeezed Jason's knee. There was a tenderness in her touch that startled him.

"We spoke with Mr. Millstone's family to get their reaction." The Millstones' living room materialized on the screen. Sarah, Paige and Jeremy sat on the couch.

"There we are!" Paige squealed with delight while pointing unnecessarily toward the TV.

"Shh," Julia sniped. "We can see, can't we?"

"Obviously, we're all very proud," television-Sarah said, putting an arm around each child. "Jason's always been a hero to this family, and now the whole city gets to see it, too." She hesitated for a moment, dropping her eyes slightly and taking in a deep breath. "I'm so thankful that we're together!"

Jason looked at his wife, perched in the recliner. She was weeping openly now, staring back at her television image with a sincerity that filled him with a horrified regret.

Back on television, the camera shifted to Paige, who was clearly nervous. "I'm very proud of my dad," she said, fidgeting with the hem of her sleeve. "He was really brave, and I'm glad the boy is going to be okay."

Next came Jeremy, who was clearly not nervous. "This is really awesome," he said. "It mostly makes me thankful that God gave me my dad instead of some other guy." Sarah and Paige laughed at this comment, along with several people outside of the camera's view.

Feeling a need to justify himself, Jeremy spoke words that froze Jason's world into a single moment of pure self-hatred: "I mean . . . I don't have any other friends who have a hero for a dad."

Those words taunted Jason for the rest of Ms. Perez's story, refusing to be distracted or displaced. They refused to let up their assault even after Jason fell into a fitful sleep later that night.

CHAPTER 6

THE ROSE

———

Jason Millstone, you are a crazy, crazy man," Travis Ellison confided to his friend at their little round table in the far corner of the company cafeteria. A week had passed since Jason's meeting with Mayor Chambers.

"That's the only thing I can think of to explain all this," the big man continued. "You are mentally unwell!"

"Thank you for your assessment, Dr. Ellison," Jason answered dryly.

"No, no, no," Travis countered, waggling a cucumber-sized finger back and forth in front of his face. "Don't start getting sarcastic with me, kid. Not unless you can give me another explanation for your recent behavior."

Sighing with frustration, Jason said, "I didn't say your assessment was incorrect."

"You see!" Travis roared, looking around the room as if gathering supporters for his cause. "Would a normal person say something like that?" Focusing back on Jason, the big man scrunched his face into a momentary spasm of concentration before asking in a more serious tone, "You're not really thinking about turning down this promotion, are you?"

Jason was not about to get into the real reasons why he felt the way he did. His lack of explanation had left Travis, who was doing his best to unravel the mystery, trapped in a state of confusion.

Jason sighed again, this time letting his head droop down until it rested on top of his fist. "Yep!"

"But, Jason," his friend whispered, "all they want to do is make you lead salesperson. That means more money, more vacation time, a better parking space—but not more work! You won't have to do a cotton-pickin' thing different!" Jason didn't answer, and Travis continued to stare down at him with increasing concern. "Well . . . frankly, kid, I think you're making a mistake. You're a heck of a poker player, I'll give you that, but what on earth are you holding out for?"

"Sheesh, Travis!" Jason cried, snapping his head up out of his hands. "Don't you get it yet? I don't have a problem with *what* they're offering. I have a problem with *why* they're offering it! Okay?" After an extended pause, Jason added, in a softer tone, "It's all because of that little boy and his opportunistic mayor of a father and that stupid award they gave me."

Now it was Travis's turn to sigh. "So that's what this is all about," he moaned. "First you turn down an interview with *Good Morning America*, and now you're going to turn down a plush promotion—all because of some weird guilt you've got stored up over something that happened . . ."

"It's got nothing to do with guilt!" Jason quickly shot back. *Wow . . . that was dumb,* he thought to himself. *It has everything to do with guilt.* He stood up with a jerk and patted Travis on his massive shoulder. "Hey, I've done nothing to feel guilty about, you got that?"

"That's exactly my point, kid!" Travis countered, spreading his hands apart in a conciliatory gesture. "You did the right thing, and now you're getting a few pats on the back thrown your way. You've gotta grab 'em while there here, my friend, because they won't stick around forever."

Looking around, Jason noticed that most of the people in the cafeteria were watching him. Leaning forward, he then spoke through tightly clenched teeth: "Look, I'm doing a lousy job explaining what's happening. So cut me some slack, okay?"

"Hey, that's fine," Travis replied, nonchalantly wiping his hand across his face. "If you want to screw up a great opportunity, you can be my guest. Just don't come crying to me when you finally open up the sugar jar and there's nothing left."

"You got it," Jason answered coolly. He gathered up the remnants of his lunch with short, aggressive jerks and turned to leave.

Aware of the eyes still watching him from around the room, Travis casually looked back while doing his best to appear nonplussed. Showing no emotion, he wrapped his super-sized hands around a mammoth roast beef sandwich and pulled it toward his face. Looking up, he was surprised to see Jason standing in front of him once again.

With a long overdue smile, Jason reached into his thermal lunchbox, pulled out a semi-smashed Twinkie, and tossed it over to Travis, who beamed and muttered, "Crazy guy!" before returning his attention to his sandwich.

Jason's mood was still dour as he pulled into his driveway several hours later. After opening the garage door, he spotted a small mountain bike abandoned on its side to the left of Sarah's van—exactly where he intended to park his car.

He sat and stared at it through the windshield for several moments, muttering, "Stupid office party. 'Congratulations on your promotion, Jason, blah, blah, blah.' Congratulate yourself, you little dweeb." Then, as if startled out of a trance, his back stiffened up like a board and he slammed the gearshift into park.

Still muttering unintelligibly, he climbed out of the car and made his way toward the front door, kicking an abandoned basketball in the middle of the sidewalk. It spun off his foot and smashed into one of the dusty millers that Sarah had planted as a border around her flower garden.

"Darn kids leave everything lying all over the yard," he hissed before pulling open the screen door. Once inside, he headed straight for the living room to search for his son, but Sarah intercepted him in the hallway.

"I thought I heard your car."

Sarah reached out and hugged him in an overly sweet way that made Jason grimace. He hugged her and thought for the hundredth time that week, *How are you doing this? Hypocrite! How do you keep acting as if everything is okay?*

"Travis's wife called a few minutes ago," Sarah continued, not noticing Jason's twisted face. "She said you got promoted at work today! Is that right?"

Summoning all his willpower and control, Jason beat the tiny muscles of his face back into a respectable façade, and then lifted his eyes to make contact.

"Yeah, they bumped me up a little bit, but it's no big deal. Basically I just get a new title, Lead Salesperson, no new responsibilities or anything, you know."

"Does it come with a raise?" Sarah asked.

"Yeah, yeah, a little one," Jason conceded, trying to sound as casual as possible.

"Well that's great!" Sarah threw her arms around his neck and pulled him close again. "We're going to celebrate with a special dinner tonight. I made BBQ chicken again!"

"Wow, thanks, honey. That's . . . that's really great."

Something about the strained quality of her husband's voice caught Sarah's attention. Only then did she notice that his back was stiff and straight and his arms were clamped rigidly to his sides like a soldier awaiting inspection—he did not hug her back the second time.

She pulled away and began a spousal full-facial scan. He met her gaze for only the briefest of moments, then looked down at his briefcase and pretended to adjust the handle.

"Sweetheart," she said, touching his shoulder gently, "we won't be ready to eat for another half an hour. Why don't you go upstairs and get a little nap?"

Jason's eyes snapped back to meet hers, but this time his face was covered with an expression of pure gratitude. "Yeah, thanks, honey. That's a good idea." With one final awkward smile, he pulled himself up the stairs and went into the master bedroom.

Watching him go, Sarah's hands moved instinctively to her hips, and her mouth puckered with curious anxiety. After a moment, she shrugged her shoulders and, with a final toss of her hair, glided back into the kitchen.

Thirty-seven minutes later, Jason staggered into the dining room with the right half of his hair sticking out at an odd angle. With red eyes blinking rapidly, he looked like a bear coming out of hibernation. While Sarah handed over utensils and dinnerware, Jeremy and the girls busied themselves with setting the table. There was a spark of enthusiasm in the air.

Jeremy and Paige temporarily deserted their work and rushed to Jason, yelling, "Daddy!" Jeremy clamped himself around one of his legs, hugging him fiercely. Adding to this unprecedented show of emotion, Julia did not exhibit her usual scowl or frown. She pulled her chair out from under the table like an ordinary person and said, "Good job on the promotion, Dad."

Jason stared at her for a moment, mouth open, before stammering, "Tha . . . thanks, Jules."

Sarah was radiant. "Let's get started," she said. "I know we're all hungry." Jason felt a bit encouraged as he considered this show of affirmation. In spite of the Millstones' dysfunction, they all wanted Jason to succeed.

Watching his youngest child meander back to the table, Jason took one more mental diagnostic before sitting down. *I'm okay*, he thought, *just needed a little rest. If I can make it through this meal, I can go back upstairs and read. No news broadcasts tonight . . . no parties . . . just a normal evening at home.*

Thus decided, Jason sat down, smiled at his family and asked, "Who wants to say grace?"

"I will!" Jeremy answered. He folded his hands in front of his face and bowed toward his mashed potatoes. "Dear Lord, thank You for this day. Thank You for the good food Mommy made us. And thank You most of all for my dad becoming a hero. Amen."

Jason winced at this last statement but relaxed almost as quickly. He did not feel the familiar guilt and shame start to build up in the back of his throat. He did not feel the simmering anger of the past week begin to boil over inside his gut. He did not feel that cold, oppressive sense of unworthiness settle over his mind like a wet blanket. What he felt was . . . nothing. *Nothing is very good! Maybe I just needed a nap,* he reasoned, grinning in spite of himself. "Thanks, Jeremy," he said, flashing an appreciative smile in the direction of his son. He turned his attention to the chicken in front of him and began to eat voraciously. His appetite was back!

All continued to go well throughout the first half of the meal. Sarah talked about the sales she discovered during a recent trip to the mall. She went on to mention several new outfits purchased so that she could have something new for the next interview.

Jason remained unaffected. "That's great news, honey," he said, helping himself to another piece of chicken. "How's your soccer, Paige?

"Yesterday was the best soccer practice ever!" Paige exclaimed. "Coach Sanders said that I could be the manager of the whole team."

"Really?" Jason asked. "What does that mean?"

"Well," Paige answered, holding up a fork in her right hand, "it means that I get to be in charge of all the equipment—cones, balls, shin-guards, that kind of stuff. But the best thing is, I don't have to play goalie anymore!"

Jason and Sarah exchanged a knowing smile before he said, "That's great news, Paige. I'm really proud of you."

"Oh!" Paige continued, pointing her fork at her father with a smile, "I almost forgot. He gave me a whistle, too! He said, 'Anyone with a hero for a father should be able to toot their own horn.'"

The entire table broke up into laughter. "Excellent news," Jason responded, cheerfully pouring a large glass of water. He smiled at the bobbing ice cubes.

"Yeah," Paige agreed, "I can't wait to show Grandma and Grandpa tonight!" There was a sudden intake of breath around the table as Jeremy, Julia and Sarah gasped.

"Paige," Julia shushed her sister in an accusatory whisper.

Jason looked at Sarah, puzzled. "Your folks are coming over tonight?"

Sarah groaned. "Oh well, it was supposed to be a surprise, but since the cat is out of the bag . . ." she slapped Paige playfully on the hand, "I guess we'll tell you. Mom and Dad didn't get to see you on the news last week."

"They were playing Canasta," Julia added, a look of righteous indignation plastered across her face.

"Anyway," Sarah continued, "Mom's been asking to come by all week, but we haven't been able to organize a time. But then, when I heard about your promotion today I thought, Why don't we have a party here tonight and celebrate?" An unseen cauldron deep in Jason's gut began to boil. His carefully maintained smile slowly began to morph into a grimace. His eyes narrowed into thin, unfeeling slits. No longer looking at him, Sarah didn't notice. "It's perfect timing, you know?" she continued. "I mean this is the one-week anniversary of you becoming the city's first hero and . . ."

"No," Jason interrupted. Something heavy and ice-cold wrapped itself around his mind and pressed down.

"Wha . . . ?" Sarah spluttered. "What was that?"

"No!" Jason repeated. "No more news broadcasts. No more parties, not even with your parents." His voice was low, almost a whisper, but was as cold and sharp as a whetted knife.

"Oh," Sarah hedged, "well, it's not really a party. I just thought . . ."

"I know what you thought," Jason cut in, "and I need you to start listening. I'm worn out from all this publicity. I can't take any more parties, and no replays of that interview, okay?"

"Geez, Dad," Julia chided, scornfully, "what's the matter with you? Mom just wants to have a little fun because she's proud."

"Stop talking, Julia." Jason swiveled his head toward his oldest daughter and locked into place an icy, unblinking stare. Julia jumped up and fled the dining room, screaming an obscenity that she had not learned at home. Everyone else sat in a momentary state of horror at Julia's vocal display. Sarah finally broke the silence.

"Kids, why don't you take the dishes to the kitchen, okay?"

"No, no," Jason called out as they began to move. "You kids need to hear this, too." He stood up and grabbed the back of his chair with both hands, his voice no longer emotionless. "From this point forward, no one in this house will mention what happened last week on the Lake of the Ozarks. No one will mention that I received an award from the city of Midland. No one will mention the times I have been on the television. And no one will mention my promotion at work. Does everyone understand? Good."

The remaining members of his family quietly stared at him as if they were looking at a madman, each face etched deeply with marks of surprise, confusion and shame. None of Jason's behavior made any sense.

He went to the fridge and rummaged for a diet Coke. As he closed the door, a flash of color caught his eye. Turning toward it, he spotted a sheet of paper stuck to the fridge with a round, black magnet. It was a picture, drawn with a combination of crayons and colored pencils. It was Superman. The superhero was suspended in mid air over an average looking house, bright red cape fluttering in the wind. The artist had paid special attention to the gold S on his chest, which was outlined against the sea of blue by a crimson shield.

As Jason examined the picture more closely, he discovered that it was not Superman. The facial features on the drawing were similar to his own, and the two shared the same haircut. Clutched in the iron grip of the man of steel's right hand was a black leather briefcase. The word "SuperDad" was scripted across the top of the page with the name "Jeremy Millstone" signed on the bottom right corner.

Jason's last thin wire of self-control snapped with a visible twitch of his neck and head.

"Jeremy!" he roared, ripping the drawing away from the fridge and turning back toward the table. The magnet skittered across the kitchen floor as if trying to escape an approaching storm. "It's time for you to stop this nonsense!" He advanced toward his son, but Sarah stood up in front of him.

"Jason," she pleaded, "I don't think this is the right time to . . ."

"Butt out, Sarah!" Jason barked, but did not try to push past her. Instead, he looked down at the boy and yelled. "No more leaving your bike lying in the middle of the garage, no more toys cluttering up the sidewalk, and no more pictures of me as superman!" He crumpled up the paper in his fist as he delivered the last line. "Do you understand?"

His young son couldn't answer. "Do you understand me, Jeremy?"

"Yes . . ." the boy was devastated. Tears gushed from his eyes as he began to cry.

"Good," Jason answered. "And that applies to all of you."

He twisted his head around to Sarah and Paige. "I am not a hero, okay? I want to be treated like a normal person because I am a normal person. And we're a normal family, so we're going to act like one from here on out." After a very awkward, very silent pause, he said, "I'm going upstairs to watch some TV."

Without another word, he tossed the wadded-up picture onto the table in front of Sarah, retrieved his Coke, and walked away feeling downright miserable. *What a jerk!* He said to himself as he climbed the stairs. *And a bully too!*

An hour passed before Sarah summoned up the courage to knock tentatively on the door of her own bedroom.

"Jason?" she called, but there was no answer. Making sure to remain as quiet as possible, she slipped into the room and glided over to the long, shuddering lump lying prone on the bed. Kneeling next to her husband, she pulled away the pillow covering his face.

He was not sleeping. His eyes were open, but vacant, as if he searched for something far way. Tear lines ran down both cheeks. Tenderly, she traced a finger across the curve of his exposed face, noticing the hot, damp skin.

"I don't know what happened," he pined, his voice muffled and weak. "I don't know what's happening to me that would make me do that. I don't know what's been happening to me all week."

"But, Jason, this has been the most exciting week of your life."

"I think it's been the worst week of my life, Sarah, because I don't deserve any of it. I'm not a hero. I *wish* I were a hero to our children, but after tonight, that seems fairly remote."

"Oh, honey," she breathed, now rubbing his back. "What's happened? Whatever is bothering you, why don't you tell me about it?"

"I'm sorry, Sarah," he replied, shaking his head, "you just wouldn't understand. Nobody could understand except . . ." *except Anita*, he thought. *Oh, man! I was an inch away from saying her name out loud!* "I don't think I can explain my feelings," he finished, rolling over on his back to avoid his wife's gaze. "I know what I did tonight was wrong, Sarah, and I promise to make it up to you and the kids. But what I said was the truth."

He looked back at her, trying with all his might to communicate the importance of his next statement. "I'm just not a hero, Sarah, and I have no idea how to become one. And it eats me up inside when everyone keeps talking about it. Maybe if everyone stopped talking all the hero talk . . . especially Jeremy. There have been times this past week when he looked up at me and I could tell what he was thinking, you know? He was thinking, 'I want to be like my dad when I grow up.' And I know it's all because of that oversold Hero of Midland campaign, and I just can't take it anymore. I really need you to talk to him."

"Follow me," she finally said, hopping to her feet.

"What?"

"I want you to follow me," she repeated, then walked away from the bed and stood by the door. Jason slowly rolled out of bed and followed her out into the hall. She took him by the hand and together they entered Jeremy's room.

"Where are the kids?" he asked as she opened one of her son's dresser drawers. Out came a large, red notebook.

"They're doing their homework in the living room," she answered, laying the notebook out on a small desk. "Look at these."

Jason leaned over the desk to get a closer look. As Sarah opened the notebook, Jason was immediately confronted by another depiction of SuperDad, this one flying over what appeared to be a farm of some kind. Unable to suppress a grimace, Jason looked up at his wife.

"Keep going."

Jason reached down and flipped the page. The next picture was a very accurate portrayal of Spiderman, complete with red-and-blue costume. Like SuperDad, however, the web-slinger sported Jason's haircut and carried a black leather briefcase in his left hand.

Jason turned to the next drawing. This time it was the Incredible Hulk in all of his lime-green splendor, yet once again with Jason's face. The huge muscles of his right arm were flexed in a bodybuilder-type pose, but the left arm was extended skyward. At the top, clutched between superhuman fingers, was a large sheet of paper with the letters "VHI" scribbled in bold print.

"He's still not exactly sure what you sell," Sarah chuckled, pointing toward the mysterious sheet, "but he knows it has something to do with paper."

"Huh," Jason grunted, continuing to flip through the notebook. Captain America, Wolverine, the Flash, Batman . . . each page featured a spectacular drawing of Jason as a superhero.

"Well," he said after reaching the end, "I thought I felt as low as a man could feel back in the bedroom, but I guess you've thrown me a shovel."

Sarah smirked. "Get ready, then," she smiled, "because I'm about to send down a jackhammer." With a look of mingled pity, disgust and mischief, she threw a crumpled wad of paper into his lap. "Open it back up."

Jason did so. The creased, crinkly visage of SuperDad stared back at him, his chiseled face full of accusation. *You'll never be like me*, it said. *You'll always be a fake.* "Sarah," Jason began, "I'm really not sure what you're hoping to . . ."

"Flip it over."

Feeling confused and a bit annoyed, Jason turned the paper over. At first he saw nothing but a wrinkled shadow of the picture on the other side, but then his eyes wandered over a smudge of blue.

"September 10, 2006," Jason read. He looked up at his wife, more puzzled than ever. "That was last year."

"Exactly. Look at the others."

Jason thumbed back through the notebook, this time scanning the reverse side of each page. "April 25, 2006," he read. "December 2, 2005. November 23, 2004. February 13, 2004 . . ." He met Sarah's eyes again. "I don't know what this means!"

The realization hit him with hurricane force, and he winced from the sheer weight of the discovery.

"What it means," Sarah said, "is that your son does not think you're somebody special because of some stupid piece of metal that the mayor hung around your neck." She reached down and pulled Jason's head forward, locking his eyes onto hers before delivering the knockout blow. "What it means is that you've always been your son's hero."

A single tear rolled down her husband's left cheek. He pulled in a shuddering, stilted breath and held it for what seemed like a full minute. Then, in a bright flash of unfelt pain, what was left of Jason Millstone's trembling heart broke in two.

Sarah fought for her husband that night. She led him through the valley of deep despair to a place of hope. Before long, they found themselves on their knees before the Lord, praying for their family, their children and their marriage.

* * *

The next day, Jason drove into the gravel parking lot of Stacey's Sizzlin' Grill. After finding an empty space, he pulled himself out and began shuffling slowly, painfully, toward the entrance. To the other customers walking across the gravelly square in hopes of enjoying Stacey's trademark buffet lunch, Jason sported the look of a man who had been trampled by a herd of buffalo and then punched in the gut for good measure.

Once inside, he looked wearily from booth to booth in search of his appointment. *I should have told him to bring a red rose*, he thought grimly. He caught a flash of motion in a booth next to the kitchen entrance. A man half-standing, half sitting, waved awkwardly.

Jason returned the gesture and then dragged himself down the narrow aisle. After slumping into the booth opposite his companion, he extended his hand. "Thanks for agreeing to see me, Pastor David."

"My pleasure," Pastor David replied, taking Jason's hand and shaking it. "When you called this morning, you said it was an emergency . . . and by the way you look right now, I believe you."

"Well, I guess that's something," Jason answered with some resignation. To Pastor David, his voice sounded hollow and flat, like a man speaking through some kind of primitive phone system made of tin cans and string.

Before they progressed further into their conversation, a large, loud waitress intervened. "Name's Darlene," she announced. "What can I get you gentlemen?"

Pastor David ordered Stacey's World Famous Buffet, while Jason asked for a plain baked potato with butter on the side.

"You boys wanna try our flavored iced tea?"

"No tea, just water." Jason croaked, cowering into the cushions of the booth.

"I'll stick with water, too," Pastor David added. Darlene gave Jason a thorough look before gathering up the menus and swinging through the kitchen door.

"Well," Pastor David said, "why don't we get down to business. You said your family was in the middle of an emergency?"

"That's probably an understatement, Pastor. Let's call it a major moral crisis."

For the next fifteen minutes, Jason poured out the details of his online relationship with Anita Brownlow, aka Sarah Mill-stone. "I'm not sure just how we connected," Jason reflected. "I guess I just clicked on one of those crazy pop-up ads about connecting with other people. Sarah must have clicked on the same ad another time. But, from the very first e-mail, I became convinced that I had finally found the woman of my dreams. She understood me, thought like me, shared many of the same interests and even dreamed of taking long walks on deserted beaches as the sun slowly disappeared over the horizon."

Pastor David listened with rapt attention, only looking away when Darlene returned with Jason's potato.

When Jason finished explaining Anita's request to meet and their red rose arrangement at Ozzy's Lakeshore Steakhouse, he paused for a moment to take several gulps of water. Then, after a long, deep breath, he continued, "That's when things started to get interesting."

With brutal, unflinching honesty, Jason relayed the details of that fateful day—from the hopeful expectation of his time in the booth to that last, horrible glance through the window when he finally saw that blood red rose clutched between his wife's fingers.

After his companion stopped talking, Pastor David placed his hands on the table and leaned back against the booth with a long, low whistle. "I can honestly say that I have never heard of anything like this before." The pastor laughed and added, "I can also honestly say that they never taught us this in seminary!"

Jason said nothing. He poked his untouched potato for a few seconds before letting his fork clatter down onto the plate.

"And that was the same day you rescued the mayor's son?"

Jason nodded. "But you know, Pastor . . . I learned that day that God is sovereign. I mean, He allowed me to spin my own web only to be caught in it. Yet, He had me in just the right place at the very moment the son of our mayor went under." Pastor David continued to listen, letting Jason talk it through. "Now, here's the amazing part. Sarah really is the woman of my dreams. I was too stupid, too self-focused to see it. My own ambition to get ahead at all costs and my stubbornness to always be right drove a wedge into our relationship. We both stopped building our marital house and eventually it fell into a state of disrepair."

Silence followed as the young pastor chewed a bite of steak. Jason watched him with a mixture of hope and dread. At length, Pastor David put down his knife and fork and asked, "So, what exactly do you want me to do?"

"I'm sorry?" Jason asked, taken off guard a bit.

"What is it that you want? What were you hoping to achieve by meeting with me today?"

This was not a question that Jason expected his companion to ask. "Well, I mean . . ." he began. "I guess I don't know exactly what I want to happen. I've just been feeling so bad all week—so . . . broken, you know? Like my whole world has been blown off course." He ran his hands across his face a few times before continuing. "I guess . . . well, I guess I figured that if anyone could help straighten me out, it would be an honest man who loves the Lord. So I called you."

"Tell me about feeling broken," Pastor David said, buttering half a dinner roll.

Jason started with the guilt—that horrible, suffocating guilt that clamped down on his stomach like a vice when he saw Sarah through the restaurant window with a rose in her hand. The guilt continued as he walked away from that beach on the Lake of the Ozarks and heard Jimmy's older brother call out, "Thanks, mister!"

He told Pastor David about his coworkers the next day—how they all wanted to get his version of the story, but he couldn't, just couldn't, talk with them about it. He talked about the visit from the mayor, the phone calls from TV producers and watching himself on the news night after night. He expressed his desire to be a hero to his wife and children and his sense of utter failure.

As Jason poured out his heart, something unusual began to happen: He started to feel better. *Confession is certainly good for the soul,* he thought. The cold, wet knot surrounding his heart began to loosen and fall away. The fire in his gut sputtered. And the stifling, suffocating blanket of his own sense of worthlessness lifted.

The physical effect of this release was immediate. He settled back into the cushions of the booth. His shoulders relaxed, taking pressure off of his neck. His hands, which had been restlessly moving from his knife to his napkin to his glass of water in an endless repeating loop, relaxed and fell into his lap.

Jason finally arrived at the events of the night before. He stopped for a moment to cut open his potato, spread a little butter along the top, and watch it melt down into the crevices before smashing it into a heap of fluffy, white starch.

"I really blew a fuse last night at home. Sarah made this great dinner and the kids were so excited to see me . . . and I just snapped." Between bites, he told Pastor David about his explosion at the table, about the party and the picture of SuperDad staring back at him from the refrigerator door. Then, with tears welling up in his eyes, he shared about Sarah's revelation inside Jeremy's room. "Man, that was it," Jason whimpered, pushing his empty plate toward the center of the table. "When I saw the dates on the back of those pictures—when it hit me what they really meant, you know?—I was done. I just wanted to crawl in a hole and die."

"I'll bet you did," the pastor responded, pushing his own plate aside and folding his hands on top of the table in front of him. He closed his eyes for a moment and pursed his lips in and out in deep thought. A moment later, he said, "The good news is, I think I can help you!"

"What's the bad news?" Jason asked.

"I'll tell you that in a minute. First of all, you need to know that what you are experiencing is proof that God really loves you."

"How's that?" Jason asked, not quite believing the pastor's statement.

"You were under heavy conviction. The Holy Spirit refused to let go of you. All that guilt and anguish is really quite similar to experiencing physical pain when some part of your body suffers. The pain is shouting loud and clear that something is wrong! The storm you are going through and all that distress happens to be quite common to all believers in Jesus Christ. Here's the fascinating truth about storms. They drive us to God. My dad once told me that a smooth sea never made a great sailor."

Jason had a puzzled look on his face. "I'm confused. Are you saying that God uses crisis to bring us closer to Him?"

"Absolutely! God wants our undivided attention. That's a tall order in this day and age. He wants His children to experience His love and grace. He desires for His children to walk with Him in righteousness. He even promises to chastise us in order to help us achieve His divine purpose, according to Hebrews 12." After a pause, Pastor David continued, "Let me give you a glaring example of what I am saying: Take your relationship with Anita Brownlow. Everyone is looking for that kind of a connection with someone. We are all looking for that kind of understanding and acceptance. It's hardwired into what makes us human. Does that make sense?"

"Yeah, we're all looking for love."

"More than that, Jason. We are relational creatures made in the image of God. We long for acceptance and understanding.

But here's the problem. We look in all the wrong places! That God-sized hole in every one of us can only be filled by God Himself. But here's what is most amazing: For believers who desperately search for acceptance and understanding in temporal things, God's sovereignty allows storms to blow them back to the center of His will. So, has the Millstone family experienced some storms lately?"

Both men laughed.

"Jason, have you figured out what the bad news is yet?" Pastor David asked after Darlene collected the bill and returned with the change.

Jason sighed. "I think so. But, are you sure that's the only way?"

Pastor David nodded in agreement.

"Okay, then." Jason reached across the table and vigorously shook the pastor's hand. "I really appreciate your help. Please pray! I'll let you know how it turns out."

Twenty minutes later, Jason was back in front of his desk at Van Hutchinson's Investments, Inc. Wielding his mouse with a practiced hand, he clicked his way back into his private e-mail account.

A moment later, he clicked on a subject line nestled deep in the inbox. The message was titled, "Why . . . Andrew? Why?" Jason had read it before—at least a dozen times alone, the day Mayor Chambers visited—but this time he skimmed through it. The raw pain lacing each of Sarah's words filled him with an unquenchable desire to end her sorrow—to make things right.

He clicked a button marked "Reply" and began to type.

Anita—

Before I say anything else, please know that I am sorry. I am so, so sorry for the pain you are feeling now. I hope you can believe me when I say that I feel it, too. I feel it this very second.

I know that you want answers and you deserve them.
I will give them to you, but not like this. All I can say is
that I wanted desperately to meet you that day more
than a week ago. I wanted to see you very badly, but there
was a good reason why I could not. And there is a good
reason why I have not written until now. I know that
must be hard for you to believe, but I need you to try and
trust me, Anita. If you ever felt like you loved me, please
trust me now.

The reason I am writing this is because I want a second chance. I would like to meet you face to face, Anita
Brownlow. I will explain everything.

Will you meet with me? Please say yes, Anita. I need
you to say yes, because I care deeply. Is that hard for you
to believe? It's true. So true.

Yours sincerely,

Andrew

* * *

Two days later, Jason piloted his Honda Accord into the parking lot of Ozzy's Lakeshore Steakhouse once again. A tremen-
dous wave of déjà vu swept over him as he stepped onto the
pavement. He leaned back against the car to steady himself. *You
can do this*, he told himself, tugging at his belt like a gunslinger
from the OK Corral. *You can do it for her.*

Even though he was 15 minutes early for their meeting,
Jason spotted Sarah's tan minivan parked by itself on the far
side of the lot as he approached the main entrance to the restaurant. *The early bird gets the worm*, he thought to himself, and then
stepped through an open door into the coatroom.

Standing in front of the old wooden door that separated
Ozzy's diners from the outside world, Jason quieted his racing

heart and prayed. *Lord, I feel caught in the biggest storm of my life. Forgive me for this terrible mess that threatens my marriage and my family. Please help me out here today. I need you to guide my heart and words. No matter what happens, though, please take care of my family. Amen.*

Holding his breath, Jason pulled open the door and stepped through without giving himself time to think about the consequences. He immediately caught sight of Sarah. She was sitting at the very same booth he was in just over a week ago, wearing that same white skirt and red, sleeveless blouse. A half-empty glass of iced tea rested on the table in front of her. "Hello, darling," Jason murmured under his breath.

Sarah didn't notice him at first. Her eyes glanced up as the door opened, but passed over Jason's face without a flicker of recognition. Then, just as she reached out to take hold of the glass in front of her, they snapped back in his direction, locking onto his features. Her mouth suddenly opened wide in shock.

Remembering his own disastrous retreat from that same booth, Jason quickly moved forward and plunged into the empty seat in front of her.

"Jason!" she breathed, her voice full of fear and surprise. "Wha . . . what are you doing here?"

Rather than try to explain, Jason pulled his hand from behind his back, revealing a freshly cut, long-stemmed red rose.

Sarah stared at it for a moment, unblinking.

"I don't understand," she said, looking up at him. When she looked at his face again, however, she gasped. The emotions filling his features—the sorrow and hope and pain and joy— took her breath away. In a single moment as sweet and horrible as a small death, comprehension dawned.

"Jason!" she cried, trying to get up.

He caught her hand and held it, tenderly. "Please walk with me," he pleaded, his eyes swimming with tears.

Sarah sat back down and tried to look at him—trying to find an explanation buried somewhere in the lines of his face. But there was too much shame in this moment of discovery and she turned her face away. Still holding her fingers with his right hand, he placed the rose on the table and turned her chin so that their eyes met once more.

"Jason . . ." she groaned, her voice choked by hurt and guilt and regret.

With a smile as soft and warm as the first day of summer, he said, "Call me Andrew."

* * *

Six weeks later, Mr. Jason Millstone and his radiant bride, Sarah, walked hand in hand down the center aisle of Midland Church. A small gathering of family and friends rose to their feet as organ music filled the sanctuary. Spontaneous applause broke out.

Pastor David Newman stood before them with Bible in hand. He could not help but smile broadly as his gaze slowly shifted to the well wishers.

"Dear friends and family, we are here today to celebrate the love of Jason and Sarah. This is not a wedding, but rather a renewal of their original wedding vows. Jason and Sarah want everyone to know that the sovereign Lord God brought them together as joint heirs in the grace of life. From this day forward they will intentionally place Jesus Christ at the center of their marriage. They choose to live their lives for His glory. We are their witnesses and it will be our responsibility to support and encourage Jason and Sarah as they now embark on this adventure of faith and obedience."

A chorus of *amens* echoed through the church sanctuary.

CHAPTER 7

FIJI

———

Sweetheart?" Jason Millstone perspired with tension. "I have a long overdue confession to make."

Jason and Sarah sat at the Starbucks table next to a noisy crowd of caffeine addicts, sipping their own vanilla-soy-no-foam-thank-you lattés.

"Confession?" The word caught Sarah off guard. Jason had become remarkably transparent and honest since their marriage renewal. He even took the time to enjoy a weekly, uninterrupted hour at their favorite coffee stop.

"Well, uh . . . I didn't tell you about my sales bonus at work earlier this year," he stuttered.

Sarah's eyes widened. "Really!"

"I, uh, was saving for an imaginary, faraway trip."

"With Anita Brownlow?"

Jason nodded sheepishly, reminding Sarah of a kid caught with a hand in the cookie jar. "Yep."

"How much?"

"Eight thousand dollars."

The silence stretched long. Then Sarah began to laugh. It was Jason's turn to be caught off guard by his wife.

"What's so funny?" Jason twisted his face to show that he didn't see the humor in such a difficult confession. Sarah reached over, placing her hands on his and gently squeezing for effect.

"Let's do it!" Sarah came alive with enthusiasm as if she had just seen a tiny glimpse of heaven.

"Do what?"

"Take our family to a faraway place!" She was on an emotional high and was not ready to come down. "Honey," she cooed, "you know how we always talk about getting away some winter? Well, let's spend Christmas somewhere south, somewhere beautiful. And I promise to take long walks with you on the beach!"

That's all it took to plant the hook and reel Jason into Sarah's vision. Paige decided the location—her class had studied the islands of the Pacific, and one country captured her imagination. It had once been home to vicious cannibals until Christian missionaries arrived in the early 1800s. Since then, people who were reported to be the friendliest on Earth had replaced those cannibals. Fiji.

* * *

Sarah stared intently at the computer monitor. Typing fingers and clicks of the mouse turned up picture after picture of the pristine islands of Fiji.

"Mmm, Fiji," she hummed to herself. "'The Fiji Islands are located in the South Pacific about a thousand miles from Brisbane, Australia.' Nice." A long day of searching travel sites revealed to Sarah why such a small percentage of Americans venture to the many islands of Fiji. "The exorbitant travel costs have much to do with it," one site warned. "But good deals can be found!"

Sarah would not give up. By her second day into the search, Sarah stumbled upon a discount package with special airfares to the capitol city of Suva, with ongoing passage to Reece's Place, a remote snorkel-and-dive resort on the island of Kadavu.

Calling the place a resort was stretching things—a quaint mom-and-pop operation was more accurate. Accommodations included eight bungalows called *bures* on the beach. The package was not cheap, but certainly much less than the five-star Sheraton Resort on Denarau Island.

Sarah printed out copies of the information, and everyone came to life as pictures of sandy beaches, turquoise water and palm trees made their way around the table during supper that evening. Jason interrupted the muddle with a suggestion, "Let's be democratic about this and take a vote. Everyone in favor raise your right hand!" Hands went up without hesitation. Jason and Sarah both smiled. "Then it's unanimous. We are going to the Fiji Islands!"

"Not to rain on our parade," Sarah chimed in, "but the tickets and resort booking have us departing on the twentieth of December. Does anyone know what that means?"

Paige beat everyone to the punch line. "We'll miss Christmas if we go to Fiji."

"We can celebrate Christmas in Fiji," Sarah reassured.

Paige reached into her memory bank of geography facts. "Fiji is below the equator. It's summertime there now."

"That's true," Sarah responded. "But Christmas happens on December twenty-fifth whether it's summer or winter."

"This trip is a once-in-a-lifetime adventure, and we need to all accept that money usually spent on Christmas gifts is going to cover our travel, lodging and food," Jason announced. Everyone agreed, but it was Jeremy who nodded with the most vigor. Sacrificing cool presents was no big deal—he hadn't given much thought to Christmas anyway.

"Can we start packing now?" he asked.

"Sweetheart," Sarah whispered while stroking his head, "we better wait a couple weeks since our flight is still a month away."

The Millstone family needed the entire month to get ready. Sarah had her hands full confirming flights and lodging and securing passports for everyone. By departure day, Sarah and Paige were almost experts on Fiji. The two of them had consumed every detail they could get their hands on relating to the inhabitants of one hundred of the three hundred islands that made up the Fiji archipelago. The others could not have cared less—they were along for the ride and adventure! Paige wrinkled her nose in disdain at the willing ignorance of the others.

Finally finished with the whirlwind of coaching, packing and prodding, the Millstone family stood exhausted at a departure gate in the international terminal. It was December 20.

"Hey, did you know that we lose an entire day on the way to Fiji?" Paige whispered to Julia.

"A whole day? How long does it take to get there?" Julia asked with a muffled moan.

"Oh, it only takes twelve hours to fly," said Paige, "but we lose a whole day because we cross the International Date Line."

Qantas Airlines 747-300B arrived at Nadi International Airport at four-thirty in the morning on the twenty-second day of December. An hour before arrival, the aircraft's cabin lights came on, followed by a gentle voice announcing a hot breakfast. An hour later the big jet coasted to a stop at the mobile ramp, everyone on board ready to charge into the day, even though the sunrise was still two hours away.

The Millstone family stepped off the aircraft and found themselves staring in enchantment and apprehension at a strange new world. While the sights and sounds were unfamiliar, the hot muggy air instantly reminded everyone that the winter of home had been replaced by summer.

Past the luggage retrieval, immigration and customs areas of the airport, two automatic sliding doors opened to reveal a small band of Fijians and Indians sent by their respective resorts and transportation businesses to fetch their assigned customers. A dark brown Fijian woman wearing a bright red *bula* dress imprinted with native flowers stood holding a placard. "Millstones" had been scratched on the front.

Julia was the first to notice. She stood motionless for several seconds, wondering why a strange lady would be holding her family name for everyone to see. She pointed the woman out to her mother, and Sarah wasted little time pushing through the surging crowd while waving to the woman. Contact! The Millstones had not only succeeded in arriving safely in a far country, but they were also now connected to Rosie's Tours.

The lady in the red dress radiated a big pearly smile and shouted, "*Bula vinaka!*"

Paige turned to the others. "That means 'hello,'" she shouted.

"How do you know that?" asked Jeremy.

"I read instead of playing GameBoy."

Four hours later, Jason and his family stood on the dock at the Royal Suva Yacht Club in the capitol city of Suva, watching their luggage soar through the air from one big Fijian man to another. The suitcases eventually made their way to the *Tui Tui*, an aged motor-sail vessel that sported thick native timber, rusting bolts and countless layers of marine paint. Jason laughed, "This beats the airlines. At least these guys know how to catch."

Sarah smiled back. "I wonder if they plan to throw us on the boat?"

The door to the pilothouse opened. A man in a soiled sea captain's hat and a white uniform shirt partially soaked in grease and oil emerged from the cabin. It was obvious that he'd been wrestling with the ship's engine. The man's experience and passion could be read in the lines of his weather-beaten face.

"*Bula!*" the man cried with a voice loud enough to raise Neptune from the depths. The entire Millstone family turned toward him as he jumped the railing and landed with a thump beside them on the dock. A thick rough hand thrust out to them. "Welcome to *Tui Tui*! Captain Jona here. I take you to paradise today!" The family boarded the ship, ready to tackle the next leg of their adventure. In only a few more minutes, the crew let go the lines and they were off.

The crystal turquoise waters within the coral reef surrounding Suva Harbor were calm, but turmoil greeted the vessel as it reached the open ocean. The stiff headwind and ominous clouds in the distance warned Jason that a storm was brewing.

"Captain Jona, how many hours will it take to get to the resort?"

"Ah, on a good day maybe twelve hours."

It was obvious to Jason that the day showed little promise of being a good one. "Okay, how many hours for a day like today?" he asked, trying to mask his irritation.

Captain Jona lifted a black coffee mug to his face, took a long swallow of cold black coffee and stuck his head out of the pilothouse window. After what seemed like a full minute, the captain turned to Jason and said with an odd smile, "Could be more!"

Frustrated, Jason turned on his heel and made his way back to the salon, where the rest of the family had settled in, trying to make the most of the pitching and rocking journey. Sarah and the children huddled in a circle on the floor, which she had decided was the safest place. As Sarah looked up to Jason, a sign of alarm etched across her face.

"Are we safe?"

"These guys do this every day of the week." Jason did his best to bring assurance and comfort, though he himself felt anxious about having his family out in stormy seas. Rather than continuing his balancing act in the wildly rocking vessel, he sprawled on the floor with his family. "Hey, let's sing some songs!"

Everyone looked at him as if he had lost his mind. All three kids were nauseous and only one short step from losing their lunches. Julia and Paige sat up and gamely started singing

"He's Got the Whole World in His Hands."

Jeremy remained flat on his back. He was in no shape to sing. His stomach demanded his constant vigilance to keep from revolting. He held his hands over his face in a feeble attempt to suppress the surging eruption. Before the others could reach the third stanza of the song, the young boy sprang to his feet and dashed for the ship's head a few feet away. He almost made it in time.

The wind's velocity increased to gale force by the twelfth hour of the *Tui Tui*'s voyage to Kadavu Island. Mountainous fifteen-foot swells slammed against the bow of the old vessel. Crew members ceased their labors to hang on with each crash of the waves. It was obvious even to the landlubbers that the situation had become dangerous. In Jason's mind, this South Seas exotic passage to one of the world's most remote resorts was becoming more ominous with each passing hour and no longer worth putting his family at risk.

As evening came and darkness invaded, the Millstone family tightened their group hug. Sarah had succeeded earlier in scrounging up several old, musty pillows, which provided limited comfort as each child made an effort to find a way to sleep on the hard floor inside a boat that pitched like a spastic rocking horse.

When he could stand it no longer, Jason forced himself to his feet and stumbled back into the control room. Captain Jona was hard on the wheel, attempting to maneuver the ship as an endless array of moving mountains of water lined up to challenge their forward momentum. Captain Jona caught Jason's movement out of the corner of his eye but made no effort to acknowledge his presence. This further confirmed the severity of the situation in Jason's mind.

"Captain Jona, how much farther do we have to go?"

"Hard to say. Maybe six hours. Maybe eight."

Jason desperately wanted to return to Sarah and the children with encouraging words.

"So, did the weatherman say it would be this bad before we left the harbor?"

Still holding firmly to the wheel, Captain Jona turned his full attention to Jason for a brief moment and said, "Don't know. Radioed Port Authority before you arrived, but they were taking their lunch."

"Did you contact them later?"

The captain smiled broadly. "Port Authority people should be back from lunch by now!"

Funny, Jason thought to himself. *It's after midnight.*

Keeping a tight grip on the wheel with his gnarled left hand, the captain reached above for the ship's radio. He dialed a number code, depressed the microphone button, identified himself with the boat's name and waited for a response. He continued the pattern until a tired voice reverberated over the cockpit loudspeaker.

"Sah! Who is this?"

For the forth time the captain shouted out his identity. Again, the loudspeaker roared. "Sah! What is your location, man?"

Captain Jona fumbled with his GPS and in an instant began to read the location coordinates. There was only silence from the only person awake at Suva Port Authority.

Finally the speakers crackled above the wail of the wind and, once more, the person back in the capitol city shouted, "Sah!" Jason made a mental note to find out what it meant. "Is this Captain Jona Yabakidrau I am talking to?"

"Eeyo!"

The Port Authority officer spoke slowly and clearly. "Captain Jona, you are in serious trouble! A category five typhoon is bearing down on you at this time."

CHAPTER 8

KAVALA BAY

———

Late in the morning of the following day, the *Tui Tui* passed through a narrow coral passage leading to Kavala Bay and found shelter. It had been a brutal voyage for the Millstone family.

The agitated officer on the graveyard shift at Suva Port Authority relayed that Typhoon Kina, with one-hundred-and-twenty-knot winds, would hit the Fiji archipelago within ten hours. Captain Jona told everyone on board that the typhoon was just more than one hundred kilometers from Kadavu, and furthermore, the seas would be too rough for the *Tui Tui* to go around the sixty-mile long island to Reece's Place on the opposite side. Kavala Bay would provide safe enough harbor to ride out the oncoming tempest.

Jason couldn't help but wonder, *If the ocean was already this violent with the hurricane still a considerable distance from the island, what would it be like once it reached them?*

The small village of Kavala nestled along the western shore of the bay. Closely built corrugated tin and thatched roof *bures* started near the water and continued up the hill.

Jason, Sarah and the children traded the relative security of the boat's salon for a closer look at the bay and village. Grateful that the vessel had survived the sea and was now slicing through the bay's relatively calm water, they made their way to the deck's railing.

The wind continued to howl, but the Millstones stood, grasping tightly to the wooden rails. In spite of the extremely dangerous hurricane headed their way, the beauty of the island was breathtaking. Everyone chattered at once as the family tried to assimilate the exotic sights.

Jason observed several men wrestling with their long wooden canoe-like punts and surmised that if they were not hauled far up on shore, the sea would most likely sink or scatter the boats.

Sarah pointed to an unpainted concrete block building that seemed to attract a flow of human activity. "That must be the village store."

Jeremy also pointed. "That must be the church!" Sure enough, a large concrete block and wood building sat in the middle of the village. A white steeple towered above the other dwellings.

"All villagers will soon go there!" Captain Jona boomed. The Millstones turned to see him standing behind them, holding a pair of old binoculars. "There be plenty of blankets, food and water in the church," the captain shouted. "Village leaders decide that one building in the village need to be storm-proof. What building is more important than the church?"

He described how skilled artisans had built the church out of reinforced concrete and large blocks. The foundation was strong and the timber, a high-density wood called *dakua*, would keep the roof in place even during a typhoon.

As the Millstones listened to the captain, they observed a group of men lifting large wooden shutters and locking them into place over the windows of the church.

The lights came on for Jason and he turned to Sarah. "Did you hear that about the church?"

"What about the church?"

"He asked what could be more important than the church."

"The captain did say that," Sarah replied.

Jason could hardly contain himself. "That church is in the physical center of the village, and I'll bet it plays a primary role in everything that goes on here." Jason continued, gaining steam. "Everyone goes to the church for protection from the storm.

Wow! I have never seen a church so relevant to its community."
Sarah hesitated to throw another word into the conversation—
Jason was on a roll. "Jesus expects His Church to make a
Kingdom impact in every community wherever it gathers . . .
This church is doing that!"

Sarah smiled at his excitement. "Shall we visit the village
and church after the hurricane?"

Jason gathered her in his arms. "Let's do it! The kids will
love it. But first we better help Captain Jona get this boat ready
to ride out the storm."

With that, Jason went to work assisting the captain and
crewmembers with the two large Danforth anchors. Captain Jona
released one of the big anchors and then dragged it until the plow-
like apparatus dug deep into the sandy bottom of the bay. One of
the crew then motored the *Tui Tui* starboard, enabling the captain
to drop the second anchor and repeating the procedure until both
anchors firmly dug in to provide maximum holding power.

For the next two hours, the temporary inhabitants of the *Tui
Tui* worked to ready the craft for major calamity. The busy time
served to keep the Millstones' minds off the coming storm.

Captain Jona remembered hearing as a child about a terrible typhoon that caused an entire wall to collapse in a Catholic
church on another island. A number of people died. As angry as
the Pacific Ocean could become, Jona was convinced it was better to be on board the *Tui Tui*, safely anchored inside the reef.
Jona also knew that hurricanes come in all shapes and sizes and
are to be respected, if not greatly feared.

Jona remained close to the ship's radio as updates kept him
apprised of the storm's direction and velocity. The glimmer of
hope that the typhoon would change course and avoid Kadavu
entirely was quashed. Hurricane Kina was no longer coming—
she was here!

* * *

Winds exceeding one hundred twenty-five knots hit the far western side of the island just after ten o'clock at night and lashed out against everything standing in their way. Trees, stripped bare of their leaves, buckled and then toppled to the ground under the relentless pressure. It was as if a long, steady explosion had engulfed the world.

Villagers on dozens of islands huddled for warmth and assurance. Most gathered in their churches, their prayers constant and to the point: "Lord, save us! Lord, spare our homes!"

Small kerosene lanterns cast the only flickering light in the churches. Few people were able to sleep. Conversation was impossible over the continuous shriek of the wind. Death and destruction waited contemptuously for anyone foolish enough to pass through the thick wooden church doors into the howling fury outside.

The full force of the typhoon reached the *Tui Tui* an hour later. Jason stood in the control room watching the ship's wind meter with Captain Jona when the storm hit with a concussion that felt like a load of bricks dumped across the roof of the ship. Fifty-knot winds increased to more than one hundred knots in an instant. Sarah and the kids screamed as the boat whipped back and forth in the raging elements. Jason steadied himself on the handrails as he made his way into the salon. It was obviously time for a group hug. There was no conversation among the Millstone family, just squeezing for support. Over the next two hours, Jason shifted back and forth between keeping watch in the pilothouse and holding his family in the salon.

Kavala Village was beginning to sound better by the moment. Jason prided himself in possessing a sharp intellect and creative mind. That's what their present calamity needed, he decided—a creative solution to minimize the present danger. They also needed to pray. *Sarah is doing plenty of that right now*, Jason thought.

"Captain Jona!" Jason bellowed over the dissonance. "Should we go to the village?"

The captain raised his eyebrows, frowned, and stared at Jason as if he had lost his mind. "Can't go out!"

"What do you mean, we can't go out?"

"Open that door!" Jona pointed to the large sliding door that led to the ship's deck. Jason moved to the old wooden door, grasped the finger grooves with both hands and pulled. Nothing happened. He tried again, this time putting his full weight behind him. Nothing. The captain roared with laughter, which only increased Jason's resolve to pry the door open. He grabbed it again and gave it his all. The door opened mere inches, and Jason found himself being sucked toward the narrow opening. Jason pulled himself away and the door slammed itself shut. The racing wind had created a powerful vacuum, guaranteeing a swift death for anyone who made it past the door.

Jason's self-reliance was shredded to bits in an instant. His plan to get everyone safely off the boat, across the water in the dinghy and into the church was sucked out the door. His family was trapped and he was completely powerless to save them. Captain Jona continued to chuckle. Jason might have taken offense, but considering the immense size and obvious strength of the man, he chose to chalk it up to Fijian humor.

Captain Jona assigned Jason the task of keeping his eyes fixed on the light left on at the village store. It was hardly visible as the boat relentlessly swung back and forth—one minute it was visible and the next minute there was only darkness as the *Tui Tui* pitched and turned. It was as if the old vessel had a mind to escape the ropes that held it down.

Jason leaned over and shouted in the captain's ear, "Why is that light so important?"

"Bad hurricane! Our anchors may pull up."

"Pull up? What happens then?"

The captain placed a finger on the nautical chart next to him. "Reef is two kilometers back. We hit, we die!"

Jason now understood his function for the night. Watch the light. Losing sight of the light meant that the anchors had fouled and the ship could no longer remain in place. The unyielding wind, coupled with an outgoing tide, would push the *Tui Tui* back to the reef where gigantic killer waves crashed. The boat would explode upon impact.

Watching the light required considerable energy as the ship continued to pitch, roll and swing. To say the light appeared as a moving object was an understatement—it danced and darted like a demented firefly. One moment the light appeared on the starboard side and a moment later Jason caught a glimpse portside. Most often, the light was not visible at all.

Jason set up his own timing pattern, which required a glimpse of the light every two minutes. He reasoned that his eyes might fall out of his head if he attempted to fixate on such an illusive object. *Better to pace myself,* he mused. It was going to be a very long night.

Typhoon Kina reached full intensity around three o'clock in the morning. Captain Jona remained at the ship's wheel, where every few moments he engaged the throttle, shifting the engine gears in an attempt to decrease pressure on the ropes and anchors.

The constant engaging of the propeller did not fail to attract Jason's notice. "Why do you keep pushing the control throttle into gear?"

"Don't trust my anchors!" the captain shouted.

The tension of Jona's rigid back and clenched jaw made Jason's heart race with fear. As reality crushed the remaining shreds of idealism, he began to tremble. The ugly realization of their predicament terrified him.

They could not leave the boat, which was slowly disintegrating, as the wind sheared off one apparatus after another. The anchors were in danger of being compromised. Nothing could be done but hold on and watch the bouncing light.

Oh yeah, the light! Jason thought. He positioned his face close to the forward window and began to search again for the tiny beacon through the torrent of an unyielding stream of water driving against the glass.

It did not appear. He tried several other windows before it dawned on him that the light could no longer be seen.

"Captain!" Jason shouted with eyes wide open in alarm. "The light is gone!"

The captain barked commands in Fijian to his first mate, who turned his attention to the GPS navigational system. A moment later, the two men stood looking at each other as if the sky had fallen, only worse. Jason did not understand a word they said, but he had little trouble reading their faces.

"Mr. Millstone," the grave captain yelled. "The Kadavu tide runs very fast. It goes out now. The tide and typhoon work together to push us out to sea. The anchors were our only hope. My *Tui* is too slow."

Jason let the captain's words sink in and thought only of his family. His beloved Sarah and their three children needed him now more than ever before. How had he led them into this disaster? Before leaving the captain and first mate to be with his family in their final moments, Jason turned and asked with fearful, brooding eyes, "How much time before we hit the reef?"

Captain Jona was not considered a compassionate man—he was a man of the sea, hardened by years of hard work. Yet tears welled in his eyes as he attempted to respond to the question. "One hour, maybe less."

Jason left the control room to hold his family before the sea took them all away.

On the floor of the ship's salon, Sarah had managed to keep the children relatively calm. Jason could plainly see that the girls, clinging to their mother, were one short step from panic. Jeremy had fallen soundly asleep, tucked safely in one of the ship's musty blankets.

Sarah motioned to Jason to come closer. He knelt next to her and began to massage her neck. She leaned back, cupped her hand to Jason's ear and said, "I'm never going to sea with you again, buddy!"

If their situation had not been so hopeless, Jason would have broken into laughter. He struggled with whether or not to tell her that the anchors had failed and Hurricane Kina was pushing the *Tui Tui* out to sea. *Would it help? Should she know?* Jason could not find the words, so he said nothing.

All Jason's strength and intelligence could not save his family. As his hands caressed his beautiful wife's shoulders, Jason wept. A torrent of long overdue tears fell freely. The howling wind was impossibly loud, and Sarah had no idea that Jason was sobbing uncontrollably just behind her.

He did far more than cry that night. He cried out to God. He confessed his sins and the sins of the whole world. He lifted both hands high into the air and pled for mercy. He wrestled with God over his ambitions, over life's storms and over the matter of God's sovereignty.

"O Lord," he cried, "please spare Sarah and Julia and Paige and my little Jeremy. I still don't know how to be their hero!"

Jason felt torn between unspeakable fear and unbelievable faith in God. He envisioned the *Tui Tui* cracking open and spilling its invaluable human cargo onto the reef. The thought of clinging to his children as the waves tore them away was unbearable.

At four o'clock in the morning, Jason Millstone came to the end of himself. In the midst of his terrible anguish, a great peace entered his heart. Jason was amazed that a man could be so serene when his entire family was facing imminent death. There was no other explanation. It was the presence of Jesus.

Whatever came from this horrifying night, Jason knew that Jesus was enough. He wrapped his arms around Sarah, closed his eyes and drifted to sleep.

CHAPTER 9

FAMILY MISSION

———

Wake up, Millstones!" Captain Jona cried from the doorway of the salon. "We live!"

Jason jumped to his feet like a soldier who had been caught sleeping on guard duty by his commanding officer. Then—because he was still on a boat in the middle of a tropical bay and close to the back edge of a typhoon—he tumbled back down to the floor.

"How close?" he asked, getting back to his knees, desperate for an updated timetable of their doom. "How close are we to the reef?"

All around him, the rest of his family began to stir, emerging more gradually and gracefully from their rest.

Captain Jona entered the room and looked down. "Mr. Jason," he said, holding out his hands, "*we live!*"

This time, the words began to sink in. *We live?* Jason thought. "How?" he asked, looking up to the captain's awestruck face.

"I do not know," Captain Jona replied, "but Kina has passed and we remain!" He seized Jason underneath his arms and yanked him up in a massive bear hug.

By this time, Sarah was beginning to suspect that she had missed something. "Wait a minute," she said, pulling herself to her feet. "Why is that such a big surprise?"

With a sheepish grin, Jason placed one arm around his wife's shoulders and rubbed the back of his neck with the other hand.

"Well," he said, addressing the kids as well, "we hit a little snag last night. Our anchors came loose. But as sure as I am standing here, God delivered us!"

Jason explained the chain of events that should have resulted in the destruction of the *Tui Tui*—and everyone on board—beginning with his assignment to watch the light. He talked about losing one of the engines, the anchors failing and, to his surprise, about his experience with Jesus in the midst of his despair.

The family listened in solemn wonder, looking around the salon as if they wanted to be positively sure that they had really survived.

"So, what's next?" Sarah asked, looking at Captain Jona.

"First, we eat," he said. Almost instantly, there arose a collective rumbling as each of the Millstones' stomachs revved up like engines. "Then we repair damage to the boat, wait for Kina to move away and then go on to Reece's Place. We have their food! Follow me to the galley," the captain continued. "Breakfast is already prepared."

Jason and Sarah exchanged an uncomfortable look. The idea of making another trip into the open ocean was not particularly appealing to either one of them. "We'll be right there, Captain Jona," Jason replied, watching the big man duck back into the hallway and disappear. Then he turned back to face his family. "First things first," he said. "I have no idea what happened last night to stop this boat from hitting the reef, but I do know that we need to thank God for it. Let's pray."

Jeremy and Paige took their places on either side of Sarah, who put her arms around them. Julia followed a bit reluctantly, and Jason closed the circle. For the next five minutes, each member of the Millstone family expressed gratitude to God for the miraculous rescue He had provided. To Jason's delight, Jeremy also prayed for Captain Jona, his deckhands and the *Tui*

Tui. Paige added several requests for the people of Kavala village, and Sarah closed by asking for protection and quiet waters during the remainder of their trip.

After Jason said "Amen," the family followed Captain Jona through the narrow hallway into the small galley. Before Jason could squeeze into the booth, however, Jeremy turned around and launched himself into his father's arms.

"Thanks, Dad," he said, clinging to Jason as tightly as a boy can. "You saved us!"

Whether it was the ocean air or the stress of passing through a deathwatch in the middle of a typhoon, tears welled up in Jason's eyes as he said, "I'm just glad we're all here together, son."

The captain's men had covered the small table with a brilliantly colored array of fresh pineapple, sliced papaya, sizzling ham and scrambled eggs.

"Eat!" Captain Jona cried, watching the Millstones sit politely with their hands at their sides. "We have plenty . . . eat!" They pounced on the food like a pack of wolves.

After a laughter-filled breakfast with the captain, the tiny community onboard the *Tui Tui* wiped the wet windows in the galley and control room to get a glimpse of the boat and the island beyond. The combination of wind and water had stripped paint, shredded rigging and splintered wood over the ship's deck and hull. The dinghy was gone.

"I'm so sorry about your boat, Captain Jona," Sarah said.

The captain shrugged. "We live," he said. "My *Tui* can be fixed."

"Mom, Dad!" Paige yelled from the other side of the galley. Her voice was filled with emotion and concern. "Look at the village." She pointed across the bay to the windswept beach.

Jason and Sarah followed her gaze. What they saw took their breath away. Only a day before the village had been a picturesque combination of *bures* nestled within the protective bosom of the rich, green forest.

Now everything was in shambles. The splintered wreckage of homes lay scattered among the splayed trunks of fallen trees. The few remaining boats floated in the shallow waters of the mangrove trees. Villagers walked back and forth through the piles of debris, bending over every now and then to salvage a scrap of tin or wood.

Paige turned to Jason, her eyes full of tears. "We've got to help them," she said.

Jason pulled her gently into his arms and stroked the back of her head. "We will if we can, honey," he said.

He looked over at Sarah and raised his eyebrows, but she shook her head. *We can't even get there*, she mouthed.

"I don't care about our vacation," Paige continued, sobbing now. "I don't care about the resort. We've got to stay and help."

"All right, sweetheart," Jason said. "I'll talk to the captain, okay?"

As if on cue, Jona's voice rang out from behind them. "Mr. Jason," he called, "I need your help with the anchors."

"I'll be right there, Captain." Jason guided Paige gently toward Sarah. Before leaving, he lifted her chin with his hand and said, "Let's ask Jesus to make a way for us to help. He can, you know."

Jona led Jason to the front of the ship, where two thick ropes stretched down into the murky waters of the bay. One of the deckhands was already leaning over the bow.

"We pull them up," the captain announced, pointing toward the ropes. Without another word, he pulled back on a small lever located on the right side of a large square box. The ship's capstan cranked into life, winching the ropes out of the water with a rattling, screeching noise.

For the next hour, Jason and the deckhands worked to guide the two ropes, each connected to fifty feet of heavy chain, into the bow chain locker. The task was relatively easy with the ropes, but the two chains came out of the water in a single, tangled mass. Consequently, Jason got the workout of his life tugging, heaving and wrestling the chains apart. When the anchors were finally secured on deck, he sat down with his back against the railing, exhausted.

Mopping sweat off his forehead and the back of his neck, Jason dragged himself back to the pilothouse, where Captain Jona sat double-checking his nautical chart.

"Have you figured out what kept us off that reef?" Jason asked.

"No, Mr. Jason," he said. "But I will find out. But first I must make repairs." Jason stood up to follow him out of the pilothouse, but the captain stopped him with a gentle shove. "Go back to your family now."

So Jason did.

For the remainder of the afternoon, the Millstones did what they could to bring a semblance of order to the chaos on board. Sarah and Jeremy volunteered to tackle the salon, which was a disaster area in its own right. Paige borrowed several sheets of sandpaper from one of the deckhands and began smoothing out the nicks and gouges in the boat's wooden frame.

Julia did her best to hide from the others. Jason spotted her once on the aft deck attempting to take advantage of the newly visible sun breaking through thick clouds.

"Your mother's getting ready to start dinner for everyone," he told her. "I'm sure she could use a little help."

"No thanks, Dad," she replied matter of factly. "I'm on vacation."

Jason took a step forward, hands clenched at his side—and then he stopped. One step, then he sucked in a deep, mind-clearing breath. "The people on this boat saved your life last night, Julia," he said, stuffing his hands in his pockets. "But if you don't want to show them any gratitude, I won't force you."

With one final, disappointed glance, he walked back toward the salon.

After dinner, Captain Jona asked Jason to accompany him back to the pilothouse. "I have the good news and the bad news," he said, slumping into his command chair behind the main windshield.

"What's the good news?"

"I fix engine number two. It is ready to go."

"What's the bad news, then?"

The captain sighed and shook his head slowly back and forth. "Rudder hydraulic is broken. I cannot fix."

"What does that mean?"

"Without rudder, we cannot steer." Jona shrugged his shoulders at Jason with a mixture of apology and helplessness. "We cannot leave the bay until help arrives."

Jason fought to keep a smile from spreading across his face. He had been wracking his brain for a way to keep his promise to Paige, and now he was getting it handed to him on a silver platter! "How long until help arrives?" he asked.

"I radio Port Authority," the captain answered, a look of bitterness clouding his features. "They say they will bring the parts we need in one week."

Jason decided to go for it. "You know, Captain, my family and I prayed for you last night. And for the *Tui Tui*."

"You pray for my *Tui*?" Jona asked, cocking his head to one side.

"Yes, we did," Jason answered. "We also prayed for the people of Kavala . . ."

The captain lowered his head. "Very bad storm. Village in bad shape."

"If there's anything my family could do to help," Jason said, "please let us know."

The captain stared at Jason in silence for a moment, and then a wide grin stretched across his face. "Down below we have food and supplies for Reece's Place. They will go bad before we get there. Maybe tomorrow we take them over to Kavala village."

Jason returned the smile. "Sounds great, Captain Jona." He was about to head back to the salon when a thought struck him. "Oh," he said, "did you ever figure out what kept us from hitting the reef?"

The captain's eyes grew wide. "I show you!" he said, scooting over to a large instrument built into the main console. To Jason, it looked like an overgrown fish-finder. The captain flicked a couple of switches, and a row of green horizontal lines appeared on the screen.

"This is the bottom of the bay," said Captain Jona, running his fingers along the lines. They looked like the contour marks on a topographic map. He twisted a few knobs until a large, semicircular blob appeared in the center of the screen. A single line emerged from the top of the object and then trailed off the screen. Jona placed his finger on it. "This is the . . ." The captain searched for the right English word. "Ditch! Yes, the anchors came together and plowed a ditch for a mile. Only mud flats down there." He then pointed to the large object in the center. "This is the only rock in Kavala Bay. This rock saved the *Tui*."

"So that's what our anchors caught hold of?" Jason asked.

The captain raised both his eyebrows. "Yes, Mr. Jason. We are saved by the rock!"

Jason was astounded. He reached out and patted the big man's shoulder. "God is our rock!" He turned and left the pilot-house, singing, "Jesus is the rock of my salvation; His banner over me is love . . ."

That evening, after the children had gone to sleep, Jason walked with Sarah along the deck of the *Tui Tui*. Under a cloudless sky and brilliant, white-fire moon, he told her about the captain's decision to bring supplies to Kavala village and about the bus-sized rock that had saved their lives.

"This has been quite a day," she breathed, leaning her head against his shoulder.

"It has," Jason agreed, reflecting on the miraculous events of the last twenty-four hours. "I can't believe Jeremy and Paige wanted to pray again before they went to bed."

Sarah nodded. "Do you think Julia will come around?" she asked.

"I think so," Jason answered. "But I'll be honest . . . I don't have a clue how to connect."

They shared a moment of silence before Jason burst out, "I just can't believe how much things have changed! I mean, praying as a family twice in one day! When was the last time that happened?"

"That's easy. Never."

Jason lowered his head. "For the first time, I really feel convinced that God is doing something remarkable in our lives. It's taken me a long time to listen and tune in."

His wife wrapped her arms around him. "All it took was a typhoon!" she said, giving Jason a quick kiss on the cheek.

CHAPTER 10

KAVALA VILLAGE

—

Two days after Typhoon Kina abandoned the Fiji Islands to spin herself into oblivion, the Millstones awoke to brilliant beams of sunlight streaming through the salon's small windows. Still shaking off the last vestiges of sleep, Jason opened the door to let in some fresh air.

Outside on the deck, Captain Jona and his deckhands unrolled a large, yellow mass of thick rubber. As Jason watched, one of the deckhands connected a small air compressor to a valve on one of the sides, which began pumping in air.

"Paige, come here for a sec!"

Still rubbing her eyes, his youngest daughter stumbled over and leaned against her father's leg. "What's that?" she asked.

"Wait and see," Jason said. After a few minutes, there was no longer any doubt.

"It's a boat!" Paige exclaimed. "Does that mean we're going to the village, Dad?"

"It does!" Jason cried, catching her in his arms and spinning her back into the salon. By this time, the sound of the air compressor had stirred Sarah and Jeremy out of their makeshift beds. They slowly peeked out the door.

"Cool!" Jeremy said, watching the captain and his mates lower the small inflatable over the side of the *Tui Tui*.

"Come on," Jason said. "Let's see if they need any help." Paige and Jeremy were out the door before he could finish his sentence.

Before following them, Jason turned back around to address his oldest child. She was still lying on the floor, wrapped in a tangled cocoon of musty blankets. The iPod was already on.

"Jules," Jason called, speaking loudly enough to be heard over the music. She stirred a little but did not look up at him. "We're going to take a trip into the village today, so I'll need you outside in five minutes to help us get ready." Without giving her time to respond, he walked through the door and into his first real dose of tropical island sunshine.

Because of the small size of the raft, it was decided that Captain Jona and one of his subordinates would make the first trip across the bay with some supplies. Then, if everything went well, the captain would return for the Millstones and more provisions. When everything had been prepared, the captain and crew of the *Tui Tui* motored slowly across the now-placid waters of Kavala Bay. The trip took all of five minutes. The Millstones watched from the railing as the villagers noticed the boat and then congregated on the beach to welcome it with smiles and laughter and bear hugs.

"I hope they let us come, too," Paige whispered, pushing back from the railing as Captain Jona directed the unloading of the gear and supplies into a large pile on the beach.

"They sure look friendly," said Sarah.

As if in response, a disgruntled "humph" rang out from behind them. "What exactly did you need me out here for again?" Julia sneered. She looked over at Jason with eyes that would have sent Medusa heading for the hills.

"You're mother and I need your help," Jason answered, choosing to remain cheerful. "You, too," he added, indicating Jeremy and Paige. "We need to decide how to best help the villagers once we get there."

Instantly, a chorus of suggestions rang out from the younger children. (Jason also thought he heard "leave them alone" coming from Julia's direction, but he ignored it.) Holding up his hands, he said, "Whoa! Calm down. Let's take this one at a time."

"I've got an idea," Sarah announced, digging around in one of the travel bags she had just retrieved from the salon. After a few moments, she produced a notepad of paper and a handful of assorted pens and pencils, which she spread among the family.

"Take a minute," she said, "to think and pray about what would be most helpful for the villagers. Then we'll share our ideas and pick out the best ones, okay?" Paige and Jeremy had already plunked themselves down on the deck before she finished, and Jason gave his wife an admiring smile and wink. Julia sighed heavily and then closed her eyes.

When each person had finished, Sarah listed all twelve ideas on her own sheet. (It was really nine ideas—Julia's three contributions were: "Teach them to sunbathe," "Take a nap" and "Go home.") After combining two overlapping ideas, seven remained. She wrote these on a new piece of paper and passed it around the family. "Put a check next to your two favorite ideas," she said.

Once the list returned, she read aloud the most popular suggestions: "One, help pass out Captain Jona's supplies. Two, help clean up the village. Three, help the villagers rebuild their homes."

"Those are some good ideas," Jason said, standing up and rubbing his belly. "But I think we should start with some lunch."

"Me, too!" Jeremy cried, standing next to Jason and rubbing his own belly in sync with his dad.

"Finally," Julia muttered, tossing her gold-streaked hair once again.

It was half past noon before the Millstones saw Captain Jona motoring the inflatable back toward the *Tui Tui.*

"You are welcome in the village," he called, throwing a small rope up to Jason, who began pulling them close enough to board. When more of the supplies had been stowed, Sarah carefully climbed down the ladder and stepped into the rubber craft.

The children followed suit. As the last to get in, Jason pushed away from the main boat before finding a seat.

"The chief is very happy," the captain reported as he tugged on the small two-stroke engine hanging off the back of the raft. "They prepare a welcome ceremony for you at the church. Fiji tradition."

"How is the church?" Jason asked, swinging his head toward the beach. He could see the church standing resolutely over piles of debris. It had been hit hard but suffered only minor damage compared to the rest of the village.

"Did all the villagers go to the church during the typhoon?" Paige asked.

"Of course," Captain Jona answered matter of factly. "Like I say before, the church is built for bad weather." As the Millstone family craned their necks, they saw the cinder block walls and tall, proud steeple silhouetted against a tangled mass of fallen trees.

When the small craft was still several hundred feet away from shore, at least fifty villagers poured out of the destroyed village and made their way down to the beach, all clapping and singing and smiling. Jason looked over at Julia and grinned. "I had no idea you were so popular here," he said. She rolled her eyes but said nothing.

After hopping out of the boat, the family was immediately engulfed in a wave of warm hugs, handshakes and even a few kisses on the cheek. Before long, they all made their way back to the church.

Up close, Jason and his family were dumbstruck by the devastation. He had felt sorry when watching disaster victims pick through the pieces of their flattened homes on TV. He had been truly grieved by the view of this fallen village from the *Tui Tui*. But to be here—to walk in and around the splintered pieces of wood and shredded clothes—the experience tore at Jason's heart like nothing he had ever encountered.

In spite of the wreckage, the villagers remained happy. They smiled, they danced, they sang—seemingly unaware that their entire lives had been mangled. How could that be? How could they respond with joy?

Because their lives haven't been mangled, Jason thought to himself. *Their possessions have been trashed, but not their lives.*

Sensing his emotion, Sarah gave Jason's hand a gentle squeeze before they passed through the thick, hardwood doors of the Kavala church.

Inside, Jason was surprised to see that there weren't any chairs or pews. Instead, the floor was covered in thin, colorful mats, each featuring a different painted pattern.

"Those are *voivoi* mats," Paige whispered, perhaps sensing Jason's confusion. "They're made from tree bark."

"Huh," he answered, nodding approvingly at his youngest daughter.

As the family made its way farther into the room, Captain Jona put a hand on his shoulder. "That is the chief," he said, pointing to a very large man seated in the center of the sanctuary. Contrary to the movies Jason had seen featuring native islanders, the chief did not wear an outfit made from wild animal skins or carry a monstrous spear. Like the rest of the Fijians, he was dressed in a T-shirt and a long blue wraparound *sulu* cloth.

"Next to him on the right is the *Roko,*" Captain Jona continued. Jason's face must have betrayed his puzzlement, because the captain explained, "He is the village manager, second in command after the chief."

"Ah," Jason said, giving the *Roko* a friendly glance.

"And on the left is the *Tala Tala.* He is the village pastor."

"Oh," Jason said, happy to already understand this definition.

By this time, the villagers had gathered together in a large circle. Captain Jona, his deckhands and the Millstones joined in, sitting directly across from the chief and the other leaders. After everyone was seated, two of the younger villagers carried in a large, wooden bowl and set it down in front of the chief. With great ceremony, the chief began to mix a thick, brown substance that reminded Jason uncomfortably of watered-down mud.

"Are they going to drink that?" he asked Captain Jona.

"Yes," he replied. "It is called *kava*. They make it from the *yaqona* bush. You will drink as well."

"What?" Jason hissed.

"Fiji tradition," the captain whispered. "Very insulting to turn down *kava*, especially from a chief."

Jason frowned. "What's it taste like?" he asked.

Captain Jona considered this for a moment, and then chuckled. "Can't explain," he said, shrugging his shoulders apologetically. As he spoke, the chief reached into the bowl, scooped a half-coconut shell full of the foul-looking mixture and handed it to the *Tala Tala*.

The pastor clapped loudly three times with cupped hands, making a loud *whomping* sound that ricocheted off the beams. Then, in one, smooth motion, he scooped up the coconut shell, raised it to his lips, and drained its contents. After clucking his tongue appreciatively, he handed the bowl back and clapped his hands three more times. The entire process was then repeated with the *Roko*.

"Next will come the guests," Captain Jona whispered, and Jason felt a surge of adrenaline rush through his body. The chief scooped up another shell full of *kava* and handed it to his attendant. The young man extended the bowl to Jason while keeping his head below the heads of his village elders.

Jason clapped three times but with flat hands. It sounded more like a small child's clap than the thunderous impact of large Fijian hands coming together. Sarah nearly lost her composure at the puny sound—she struggled to keep from laughing hysterically. Jason received the shell with both hands, glanced in Sarah's direction and pulled it to his mouth. To his surprise, he drained the bowl. Realizing how pathetic his first three claps were, Jason clapped his hands this time with enough force to make the village dogs lift their ears.

The *kava* was not unpleasant. Up close, the mixture looked even more like mud than it had before, but it didn't taste like dirt. Strangely, the drink possessed a spicy undercurrent that reminded Jason of the small bags of potpourri his mother used to make.

It was then that Jason noticed his mouth and tongue going numb.

After yet another refill, the chief turned his attention toward Sarah. Before she accepted the bowl, Captain Jona leaned over to her and whispered, "No clap. Men clap loud enough for whole village."

In a single, spasmodic jerk, she heaved the half-shell to her lips and drank. For a moment, Jason didn't think she would make it through, but she did. Grimacing slightly, she handed the bowl back to the chief.

Looking past her, Jason noticed that all three of the children were staring at their mother with wide-eyed expressions of unadulterated awe. He smiled. *Welcome to Fiji, kids*, he thought.

* * *

"You not like many outsiders," said Ratu Timoci, chief of Kavala. The elders, Captain Jona and Jason had withdrawn to a small room behind the church. The *Roko* knelt on the chief's right, the *Tala Tala* on his left. Across from them, Jason and Jona sat cross-legged on a pile of mats with colorful fringes.

"Many outsiders . . ." the chief began, but his face clouded after a moment of intense thought. Turning to the *Tala Tala*, he spoke several sentences in Fijian.

"The chief says that you are different than most of the tourists he sees when he goes to the mainland," said the *Tala Tala*.

Jason raised his eyebrows. The pastor spoke excellent English—much better even than Captain Jona.

"Most tourists care only about tanning their bodies and relaxing their minds," he continued. "Why would your family choose to work and sweat under the sun for Kavala village?"

Jason considered this for a few moments. "My family and I are Christians," he said, looking back and forth between the chief and the *Tala Tala*. "We serve the Lord Jesus Christ and follow His teaching." As Jason pondered his next words, the *Tala Tala* translated what he had said to the chief. "After the storm, my family prayed," he continued. "We asked Jesus what He would do if He were on a boat in Kavala Bay. My family and I believe He has led us here at this time to help."

Wow, Jason thought. *Where did that come from?*

As the pastor translated Jason's answer, the chief's eyes grew large. Turning to the *Tala Tala*, he spoke rapidly in Fijian. A discussion followed between the two of them. To Jason, it seemed as if the chief were asking several questions in rapid succession, while the pastor did his best to answer them.

Finally, the chief smiled widely and gestured back in Jason's direction. "We are honored, Jason," said the *Tala Tala*, who was also grinning. "We are grateful that you serve the Lord Jesus as we do, and that He has brought you to our village. The chief humbly accepts your gracious help as well as the help of Captain Jona."

The *Tala Tala* rose to his feet as he spoke, along with the chief. Jason and Captain Jona followed suit. Before Jason knew what was happening, the chief had engulfed him in a tight, sweaty bear hug. "*Bula vinaka!*" he roared.

"You're welcome," Jason wheezed when he was released.

The rest of the afternoon passed quickly. Jason and Jeremy joined the captain and his deckhands in gathering all the usable wood they could find from among the wreckage of the *bures*. Sarah and Paige helped the village wives relocate their scattered clothing, utensils and broken furniture. Julia kept company with her iPod while participating in as little work as possible.

As the sun approached its resting place near the horizon, Captain Jona signaled Jason that it was time to return to the *Tui Tui*. Jason rounded up the other Millstones and herded them toward the beach.

The *Tala Tala* intercepted them as they approached the inflatable raft. "Good evening, Millstone family!" He turned his attention to Jason. "Will you walk with me a moment before you go?"

"Sure," Jason said, curious what this interesting man might want with him.

"You have a wonderful family, my friend."

"Thank you, *Tala Tala*," Jason answered.

His companion made a dismissive gesture with his hand. "That is a title," he said. "Very formal. Please call me Jokini."

"Okay, Jokini it is." They walked in silence for a few moments before the pastor stopped.

"May I ask you a question?" he said. "It is about your oldest daughter."

"Her name is Julia," Jason said, unable to help looking down at his feet.

"Julia," Jokini repeated. "A lovely name. Is everything well with Julia?"

Jason was surprised that the question didn't offend him. Something about Jokini made it seem almost natural. "No," Jason answered, still looking down. "Why do you ask?"

"I spoke with her today," Jokini said. "In her eyes I saw many things: confusion, anger, spite. They are a hard load for one so young to carry." Jason shuffled his feet awkwardly, ashamed at the truth of Jokini's words.

"There is no need for embarrassment," he said, "nor is there time for shame. You were brought here by our Lord Jesus to help us in a time of great need and we are thankful. But perhaps you are also in need?"

Jason nodded, unsure of what to say. *What have I got to lose?* he thought. "I'm worried that we're losing her," he muttered, "that she'll grow up before I can . . . before I can rescue her from herself."

The pastor sighed deeply. "Fathers carry heavy burdens, too. Perhaps we can speak of this again tomorrow?"

"Okay," Jason answered, glancing over as Captain Jona revved the tiny engine of the dinghy. "What time should I see you?"

Jokini smiled. "There are no watches or clocks in Kavala village," he said, "and the islanders do not bow to time as you Americans do. Come to the church when it is too hot to work in the afternoon."

"Until tomorrow then," Jason said.

"Until tomorrow," Jokini answered, extending his hand. "My friend."

CHAPTER II

PARENTING IOI

———

Jason stumbled into the pilothouse the following morning, drawn by the irresistible aroma of freshly brewed coffee. Sarah was already there.

"What's going on?" he mumbled, accepting the colorful mug she held out to him. "Where are the kids?"

"It's good, huh?" Sarah asked, gesturing toward the mug after Jason had taken his first sip.

"Yeah," Jason answered, still under the sluggish influence of sleep.

"It's Taveuni Island brand," she said. "I've seen it in a bunch of specialty stores back in the States, but Captain Jona says it's as common as water around here."

"Huh," Jason grunted, taking another large gulp. They stood in silence for a few moments as Jason allowed the brew to pull him into the land of the living. Sarah cocked her head at an angle as she watched him drink, the corners of her mouth rising into a mischievous grin, then fading back. Her eyes danced with a mystery that Jason couldn't place—as if she had a secret and was enjoying keeping it from him.

"What?" he asked when he could stand it no longer. "What's going on this morning?"

Sarah reached out and took his free hand. "Merry Christmas," she said, her mischievous grin now widening into a smile.

Jason blinked. He looked around the room as if searching for a calendar. Not finding one, he ran his fingers through his hair, blinked again, and then turned back to his wife. "Wow!" he said. "I totally forgot."

"I know!" Sarah cried. "So did I . . . and so did the kids."

"The kids?" Jason asked, incredulous.

"Yup. Captain Jona told us this morning. I asked him to take the kids below deck so they could get the suitcase with the presents—and you'll never believe it . . ." she beamed at him before continuing. "They want to take them to the village today and give them away to the children there!"

"What?" Jason gasped. "Are they even going to open them first?" Sarah shook her head. "Wow," Jason repeated, and then a thought struck him. "Even Julia?" he asked.

Sarah frowned. "Well, no," she admitted. "But I only got her a couple CDs and a carrying case for her i-thingy, and those wouldn't be much use to the village anyway."

Jason took another swig of his coffee and smiled. "So . . . the Millstones are Santa's elves this Christmas, huh?"

"Nope," Sarah said. "We're Jesus' disciples."

* * *

"*Eeyoo*, Mr. Jason!" Captain Jona called from across the beach several hours later. "The sun grows too hot. We take break now."

Wiping his brow, Jason looked up into the glaring yellow orb and nodded. The Millstones and the crew of the *Tui Tui* had motored to the island after breakfast. As soon as they had arrived, Jason had joined the village men who were already hard at work clearing away the massive amount of debris left by the storm. The rest of his family had been similarly absorbed in a variety of projects, all under the direction of the *Roko*.

Jason dropped his load of tree branches and ruined wood onto a large pile at the edge of the forest and then walked back toward the village. Most of the men had congregated under a small stand of mango trees that had somehow survived Kina's wrath. Instead of joining them, however, Jason veered toward the church.

Once inside, he saw the *Tala Tala* stretched out on the floor in the far corner of the room. He was resting on several tattered *voivoi* mats, with his head propped up by a portion of tapa ripped off the wall by the hurricane. A large Bible lay spread open next to him.

"*Bula*, Jokini," Jason said, smiling self-consciously at his pronunciation.

"*Bula*, Jason," the pastor replied. "Come and sit."

Jason plopped down with his back against the wall. He felt a pleasant breeze whisk over his sweaty face and neck. Looking around, Jason noticed for the first time that many of the church windows had been shattered.

"What was it like to ride out the typhoon in here?" he asked.

Jokini closed his eyes and sighed. "A hard night," he admitted, "but a good night—a night of prayer."

You can say that again, Jason thought. "I'm glad that God heard you and kept you safe."

Jokini grinned. "We held on to each other and the Lord and we also prayed for others."

"Really? You mean other villagers?" Jason asked.

Jokini did not answer immediately, but a knowing smile spread across his face. At length, he said, "We also prayed for those still at sea."

Something about that knowing smile clicked in Jason's mind. "Us?" he asked, gaping. "You prayed for us?"

Jokini nodded. "We saw your boat come into the bay as we prepared for the storm. All through the night, my brothers and I implored the Father to protect you." The two men sat in silence for several moments before Jokini said, "I would very much like to hear about it."

Stirred out of his shocked meditation, Jason sighed. For the next twenty minutes, he recounted the events of that terrible, wonderful night, culminating in God's miraculous intervention.

Jokini was an excellent listener. He concentrated with rapt attention, every now and then whistling or whispering "*Eeyoo!*" in appreciation of a poignant moment. When Jason finished an outline of the story, Jokini urged him to go deeper. Like an expert surgeon, he used simple questions to probe into Jason's heart, mind and emotions. When he finished, Jason felt as if he had bared his soul.

"Fascinating," Jokini whispered. "But I do not understand. Why were you so fearful for your family's life if death can only bring them to the Lord?"

Jason hung his head. The moment had finally come—the moment he had been dreading ever since his earlier conversation with Pastor David back at Stacey's Sizzlin' Grill. "I . . ." he began, still looking at the floor. "I'm not sure if my kids really know Jesus as their Savior. I'm worried that they're not Christians."

The *Tala Tala* did not seem shocked or angry, but the puzzled expression remained on his face. "Have you not taught them to be so?" he asked.

Jason sighed. "I thought I had. I mean, we've taken them to church for many years now, but . . ." Jason poured out the story of the Millstone family's recent troubles. He talked about Julia's run-in with the law and difficulties at school, about Paige on the computer and Jeremy with his video games. He even mentioned the tension between himself and Sarah but did not go into the sordid affair of Anita Brownlow. Mostly, he vented his worries and frustration that his children were not turning out as he had hoped.

Jokini did not ask any questions this time. "Now I see," he said, leaning his head back against the wall and closing his eyes after Jason had finished. "You are a good man, Jason, with a good heart. You want to lead your family—to be the 'hero,' as you call it. But you have much to learn."

Jason was not offended. "Can you teach me, Jokini?" he asked.

The *Tala Tala* opened his eyes. "Teach you what?"

"How to be a good father," Jason answered. "A godly father."

"I can only teach what I find here," Jokini answered, holding up his large, battered Bible for the first time. "Would you like to hear?"

"I would."

"Come back tomorrow, then, and bring your sword," Jokini added, giving the Bible a little shake. "Tonight I will again pray for your family. I suggest you do the same."

"I will," Jason said. And he did.

When the villagers retreated to the shade for the afternoon siesta the following day, Jason once again made his way to the church, although this time he stopped at the rubber dinghy to retrieve his Bible.

"*Bula vinaka*, Jason," Jokini cried when he heard the door of the sanctuary open. "Are you thirsty today, my friend?"

"Yes, sir," Jason answered, punctuating each word. He and the village men had begun construction of several new *bures* in the morning, having cleared away the last of the debris the previous afternoon.

"Follow me then, and bring your Bible," said the *Tala Tala*, "and perhaps we will find refreshment." He led Jason down to the beach and stood ankle deep in the gently lapping water of Kavala Bay. Jason joined him.

"Will you drink?" Jokini asked, reaching down and cupping some of the water into his hand.

"Uh, no," Jason answered, feeling a little awkward. "That's salt water."

"Oh," Jokini answered. "You desire something else?"

"Well, yes," Jason said. "Is there any fresh water? Salt water would just make me sick."

"I see, I see . . ." Jokini replied, tapping his chin in mock contemplation. "Let us try another place." He walked back up toward the church and then veered off onto a foot-worn path meandering lazily into the woods. Feeling thoroughly confused, Jason followed in silence until they stopped on top of a small hill several hundred yards away from the village.

"Perhaps this is better?" the *Tala Tala* asked. Following his gaze, Jason saw a gush of crystal water flowing out of several cracks in the rocky outcroppings just over the crest of the hill. It washed down the rocks in interweaving rivulets before pooling into a single stream at the bottom of the ravine.

"Try it," Jokini said, pointing to a small tree growing next to the source of the spring. Walking toward it, Jason saw several nails sticking out of the trunk at odd angles. A metal cup hung down from each one. Taking one in his hands, Jason dipped it into the flow of water and then put it to his lips.

"Wow!" he said after taking a sip. It was the best water he had ever tasted—pure, crisp and cool. After taking another few gulps, he replaced the cup and turned to Jokini.

"All right," he said, "I know there's a lesson in here somewhere. Why did we go down to the beach first?"

The *Tala Tala* smiled. "First, the Bible," he said. "I would like you to read the first nine verses of Deuteronomy, chapter six."

Jason pulled his Bible out of the cargo pocket of his pants and flipped to the appropriate spot. "Chapter six," he confirmed.

Now this is the commandment, and these are the statutes and judgments which the LORD your God has commanded to teach you, that you may observe them in the land which you are crossing over to possess, that you may fear the LORD your God, to keep all His statutes and His commandments which I command you, you and your son and your grandson, all the days of your life, and that your days may be prolonged. Therefore hear, O Israel, and be careful to observe it, that it may be well with you, and that you may multiply greatly as the LORD God of your fathers has promised you—a land flowing with milk and honey.

Hear, O Israel: The LORD our God, the LORD is one! You shall love the LORD your God with all your heart, with all your soul, and with all your strength. And these words which I command you today shall be in your heart. You shall teach them diligently to your children, and shall talk of them when you sit in your house, when you walk by the way, when you lie down, and when you rise up. You shall bind them as a sign on your hand, and they shall be as frontlets between your eyes. You shall write them on the doorposts of your house and on your gates.

"Who spoke these words?" Jokini asked after Jason finished. "Who wrote them down?"

"Moses," Jason answered. "He wrote the first five books of the Bible."

"And do you know when and why he spoke these words?"

Jason rubbed the back of his neck. "Uh, they were still in the wilderness, right?"

"That is correct. Moses was at the end of his life. These verses are the beginning of his final instructions to the Israelites. They are the most important part of those instructions."

Jason was not following. "But what do they have to do with being a godly parent?" he asked.

Jokini raised his eyebrows. "It was God's plan for Israel to become a great nation, yes?" Jason nodded. "The people Moses spoke to had seen many miracles from God. They were filled with faith. But what of their descendants?"

The answer clicked in Jason's mind. In fact, it now seemed obvious. "Moses' generation would have to teach their children about what God had done, and how to follow Him," he said.

"*Eeyoo*," Jokini answered. "And that is why we read today. These verses contain three commands from God to parents like you and me. They are to be the foundation stones of our families."

Jason skimmed through the verses once again. "You're going to have to help me find them," he said.

"Please read verse five again, my friend," Jokini replied.

Jason read aloud. "You shall love the Lord your God with all your heart, with all your soul, and with all your strength."

"Do you love God?" Jokini asked.

Jason was taken aback. "Well, of course," he spluttered.

"Why?"

"I . . . well, because," Jason rubbed the back of his neck again, self-conscious about his inability to articulate a clear reason. "Because . . . He's God!" he blurted out.

"Yes," Jokini replied. "But there are still many who do not love Him. Why is it that you do?" He allowed Jason to sit in an uncomfortable silence for only a few moments before continuing.

"Think about Kavala village," he said. "Our small island and the ocean beyond are the whole world to my people. Our food comes from the water. We bathe in the water. We travel on the water. But you choose not to drink the water from the ocean. Why?"

"Because it would make me sick," Jason answered. "It would kill me, eventually."

"That is right," Jokini said. "The ocean water has its place in all of our lives, but it cannot bring life. By itself, it leads to death. It is the same in America. Your job, your home, your clothes—all of these surround you as the ocean surrounds this island. They are the world in which you live, but they are not your life."

Now having Jason's full attention, Jokini turned back to the stream. "Why did you drink this water?" he asked.

"Because it's fresh," Jason said. "It won't make me sick."

"But why drink in the first place?" Jokini pressed.

"Because I was thirsty," Jason answered. "Because I need it to survive."

"Yessss," Jokini breathed, extending the word into an expansive smile. "The pure water brings life." He dipped a cup into the flowing spring and drank deeply before adding, "Just as God does."

"I believe that," Jason said.

"*Eeyoo*. He is the source of our life. I live my life in Kavala Bay—that is my world. Your world is America. But both of us have the same source of life. It is God. As awareness of God grows, and as you and I grasp the significance of our new birth in Jesus, what is the outcome, Jason?"

"Ah! It's got to be gratitude. Thankfulness. Awe. Stuff like that." Jason responded.

"You seem to see the picture, my friend. We need God's many provisions to survive, but we love Him because He gives Himself to us freely—because He sacrificed Himself to become our Living Water. Yes?"

"Yes," Jason said, nodding slowly. "I see it now."

"This is the first principle of Deuteronomy, Jason—the first principle for godly parents."

"Love God."

Jason was beginning to understand the flow of Jokini's argument. "So, the implication is that I can't train my children to love God if I don't love Him first."

"That is correct. Everything in life begins and ends with the knowledge that God is the willing source, and He loves to share Himself! If we understand that, we cannot help but love Him."

"Okay. What about the second principle?"

Jokini opened his Bible and read Deuteronomy 6:6: "'And these words which I command you today shall be in your heart.'" He looked up at Jason. "The second principle of godly parenting is the reasonable outcome of the first principle: Obey God."

Jason was silent for a moment, his face scrunched with confusion. "Really?" he asked, rereading the verse on his own. "To me it sounds like we're supposed to memorize something."

Jokini laughed. "That would be true if God commanded us to keep His words only in our minds, but the heart is different. Your heart is the center of your emotions and values. Literally, it is a vital organ that pumps blood to the body, but we use the heart to talk about our ability to reason and understand."

"I still don't get it," Jason confessed.

Once again, Jokini dipped his cup into the stream of water and held it up. "If I love this water," he said, "will I survive?"

It took Jason a moment to understand where the *Tala Tala* was going. "No," he answered. "You have to drink it."

"That is right, my friend. I must drink it. I must bring it into my body before it can bring me life." He put the cup down and locked Jason with a stare. "So how do we drink the Living Water? How do we bring Him into our hearts?"

"We love and obey," Jason answered, his voice barely audible.

"Yesssss, our obedience is the fruit of our love for God." Jokini whispered back for effect. "Jesus said, 'If you love me, keep my commandments.' That is obedience."

"Mmm." Jason started to put it together. "I think I have it. God's commands are good for us and they are to be obeyed, but we will fail miserably unless our motivation to obey is love."

Jokini handed Jason one more cup of refreshing water. "Indeed, my friend, you have it!"

"Love God, obey God," Jason said. He began to ask about the third principle when he cocked his head. The sound of hammers striking nails drifted up from the village. "The men are back at work. I guess I should get back and help. Do you think you could tell me about the third principle on the way?"

Jokini smiled. "I will try," he said. Each drank one last cupful of water from the spring, and then they walked a few paces and stopped.

"Jason, let us pass on what we have learned thus far to the realm of godly parenting. Tell me, what do your children need to see more than anything else?"

A team of horses couldn't hold Jason back. "I'm tracking, Pastor! My kids need to see me and Sarah deeply in love with God, consistently walking with Him in obedience."

"I think you are now ready for the third principle, Jason. Please read verses seven through nine again."

"'You shall teach them diligently to your children, and shall talk of them when you sit in your house, when you walk by the way, when you lie down, and when you rise up. You shall bind them as a sign on your hand, and they shall be as frontlets between your eyes. You shall write them on the doorposts of your house and on your gates.'"

Jokini listened while Jason read and then said, "The third principle of godly parenting is also rooted in loving God: Train your children."

"So this is the practical part, right?" Jason asked.

"Be careful, my friend," Jokini advised. "There is nothing more practical than loving God, nothing more practical than showing that love through obedience. Your success with the third principle is entirely dependent on your willingness to follow the first two."

Jason considered this for a moment. "Okay, I can see that. So what exactly do we teach?"

"We teach what is most important," Jokini answered. "We teach our children to love and obey God as we do."

"The first two principles," Jason said. "Man, these are all pretty well connected, huh?"

Jokini smiled. "They are truth," he said, "and flow logically from one to the next and back again, but do not get them out of balance. Parents who train their children to obey without love are Pharisees who will deeply wound and embitter them. Parents who show love but ignore obedience raise selfish tyrants who hurt themselves and others."

"All right," Jason said. They were approaching the outskirts of the village now, but Jason wanted to make sure he understood everything. "So, how do I actually do the teaching?"

"The more important question is *when*," Jokini countered. "*When* should you teach?"

Jason glanced back down at his Bible. "When I sit at home, when I walk, when I lie down and when I get up." He thought for a moment before saying, "That's pretty much all the time, isn't it?"

Jokini smiled broadly. "This is the responsibility of the godly parent," he said. "We are always showing our love for God by example and by our words."

Jason threw all caution to the wind and exclaimed, "I separated all four in my mind and now I think I see something. It seems the godly parent can hardly talk about anything else! He gets up and goes to bed like every other father, but while he is awake, his heart habitually invites the Lord into his home and into every conversation."

"Very good, Jason. Do you know what the word 'diligence' means?"

Jason paused. "Does it mean to be industrious and hard working?"

"That is right," Jokini acknowledged. "But this wonderful word means even more. Many believe this ancient Hebrew word came from the practice of sharpening a knife or sword by rubbing it against a grinding stone again and again. How does that relate to you as a father, Jason?"

As Jason thought about it, his mind drifted back to his earliest conversation with Pastor David. "First of all, it means that I take responsibility for raising my own kids," he said, his voice tinged with sadness. "I don't dump them on the church and then demand that the church develop my children spiritually without me."

"Yes," Jokini agreed. "Your children are God's gift to you and Sarah. They will not be ready to hear your words every second of every day, but there will be moments of opportunity. You must watch for them and be ready."

"Like what you did with the water?" Jason asked. "At work, we call those 'teachable moments.'"

The *Tala Tala* grinned. "'Teachable moments,'" he repeated. "I like this phrase!"

Jason glanced down one final time at the last two verses. "I think I'm still confused with putting God's words on our hands, between our eyes and on our doorposts."

Jokini reached out and took Jason's hand. "Whenever you use this hand, remember to love God. Whenever you use your eyes to look at your children, remember to love God and to teach your children to love God. And then, my dear friend, whenever you walk through the door of your home, remember to obey the Lord and to teach your children to also obey the Lord. Do you see?"

Jason took a deep breath. "I see."

Still smiling broadly, the *Tala Tala* placed his hands on Jason's shoulders and stared into his eyes. "You are a good man, Jason. You will do these things we have talked about today, and you will be a godly father to your children with His help. I know this to be true. Do you?"

"I hope so," Jason answered, wiping a tear away from his eye. "That's what I want more than anything."

Jokini smiled. "Ask God," he said, "and He will give you the desire of your heart."

Later that evening, Jason and Sarah walked hand in hand on the deck of the *Tui Tui* and sat down.

"Okay," Sarah said, "that's it. I refuse to wait any longer."

"What do you mean?" Jason asked, his voice tinged with mischief.

"Something happened today at the village," she answered. "I know that you had a talk with the *Tala Tala*, and you've been on cloud nine ever since we got back in the dinghy. I want to know what happened!"

"Okay, okay," Jason conceded, smiling. "But first . . ." He jumped from the *Tui Tui* to the inflatable, pulled a small paper cup from his pocket and leaned over the side. A moment later he came up with his cup full of salty Kavala Bay water. "Would you like something to drink?"

CHAPTER 12

WELCOME HOME

———

Two weeks after the Millstones returned from their adventure in the South Pacific, Jason and Sarah sat at their dining room table and called their three children to come and eat. Fiji remained on everyone's hearts, even as the demands of everyday life clamored to wash their memories away. Paige was the last to walk into the dining room. A glint from her eyes indicated that she had a secret.

"So, Dad," she said the moment Jason concluded his blessing on the food. "What kind of award are you getting this time?"

Jason had just started scooping out a large mound of mashed potatoes. His spoon froze in mid air. "How did you find out about that?" he asked, trying to sound casual.

"There was a message on the answering machine when I got home," Paige replied. "It was from a lady at the mayor's office. She wants you to get fitted for some kind of suit that she wants you to wear at an award ceremony." Paige cocked her head and added, "Actually, she sounded a little ticked off."

Jason looked over at Sarah, who was unable to suppress an amused grin. "Yeah," he sighed, turning his attention back to Paige. "I have to go to a ceremony in St. Louis, but I'm not sure if they plan to give out more awards."

"The government wants to publicly recognize its first batch of heroes," Sarah added, smirking over in her husband's direction. Jason frowned.

"That sounds pretty cool," Jeremy piped in, concentrating on cutting the steak on his plate in front of him. "How many people are going to be there?"

"Actually, I'm not sure, buddy," Jason answered, looking over at his son. Something about the boy's appearance made him stop. *Strange,* he thought, *he looks different for some reason.* "I'll bet there'll be a couple hundred, at least," he said out loud.

"Don't forget to count the famous people, too," Sarah added with mock indifference, but Jason didn't hear her. He was still absorbed in the mystery of his son.

Why does he look so unusual? Jason wondered, scanning Jeremy's side of the table for the third time. *What's missing?* The answer hit him: the GameBoy. After receiving it as a Christmas gift the year before, Jeremy had carried that plastic box to every family meal since, always setting it in the same spot next to his right hand so that it could be taken up again as soon as he finished eating. But tonight it was nowhere in sight. In fact, Jason realized that he hadn't seen his son playing it since the family had returned from Fiji. *I'll have to ask him about that,* Jason thought.

"What kind of famous people?" Paige asked, pouncing on the bait that her mother had cast. The question pulled Jason out of his thoughts. His head snapped over to look at Sarah, but it was too late. She was too excited.

"Well, your father will be there," she answered, solemnly tapping her chin. "And me—that makes two. Oh, and the president of the United Sta . . ."

"The president?" Jeremy and Paige screamed together, looking back and forth between their parents with eager faces.

"Yes!" Sarah cried, holding her hands in the air. "The president is going to give your father an award and it's going to be on TV!"

Immediately, the three of them were caught up in a whirlwind of conversation. Jeremy and Paige peppered their mother with more questions and Sarah did her best to answer. Watching them, Jason shook his head slowly and grinned in spite of himself. *This is going to be a long week*, he thought.

In the midst of the enthusiasm, Julia's voice blew over the conversation like a foul breeze. "That's ridiculous," she said.

Jason raised his eyebrows. His oldest daughter was sitting directly across from him at the other end of the table, pushing a carrot around her plate with an air of distraction. Her head was down and he could not see her face.

"What did you say?" Sarah asked, following Jason's gaze down the table. Her voice had a flinty edge that put an end to Jeremy's and Paige's questioning outbursts.

Julia looked up at her mother, eyes flashing. "I said, *that's ridiculous*," she repeated. Her voice was still soft, but cold as ice. "It's just stupid. Tons of lifeguards do the same thing every summer. I just don't get this hero stuff."

Jason gaped at her, his eyes wide with surprise. *Where's this coming from?* He thought. He was not offended, having raised the same objection several times throughout the "Hero of Midland" fiasco, but he was taken aback by her nastiness. Opening his mouth, he started to say something like, "I don't understand it either, Jules"—but he never got the chance.

"How *dare* you speak about your father like that!" Sarah thundered, pushing herself halfway out of her chair in order to lean forward and glare down the table at her oldest child. "He did a very brave thing, and he deserves all the praise that has come his way—and more!"

Julia pushed back from the table and jumped to her feet, arms crossed. "Maybe the president is just a big fan of *Baywatch*." Jeremy and Paige looked at each other in shock, their faces mirroring each other's trepidation.

"That's enough," Sarah declared, now fully out of her seat. "You've had a rotten attitude for the better part of a month, and I'm tired of it. Apologize to your father."

"I'm sorry!" Julia cried. "But I'm so tired of everyone pretending that everything's great all of a sudden, that everyone should be all huggy and happy just because of what happened on that boat."

"What happened on that boat was a miracle," Sarah said, speaking through clenched teeth. "God spared this family for a reason, and we need to . . ."

"God?" Julia interrupted. "*God?* It was a *rock*, Mom. Just a big rock."

"No, it wasn't!" Paige shrieked. "God used the typhoon and rock to teach us and you're not listening at all."

Julia scrunched up her face into a look of pure disgust. "Forget it!" she said, spinning around and charging out of the dining room without a look back. As she ascended the stairs, she announced, "I'm going to be on the phone with Jimmy tonight, so don't bother me." Then she was gone.

Jason looked over at his wife and raised his eyebrows again. She did the same, and they both sighed. "Who's Jimmy?"

"It's a boy from school," Paige announced. "He likes Julia."

Sarah looked over at her and Jeremy. "Huh. Hey . . . would you guys mind working on your homework in the living room for a little bit? Oh, and by the way . . . your dad and I will be spending the weekend in St. Louis for the ceremony and a mini-vacation, which means that Grandma will be staying over Friday and Saturday night with you."

Jeremy and Paige both cheered—Grandma always came with an overabundance of cookies, candy and money for activities—and took themselves off to do schoolwork.

Once alone, Jason turned back to Sarah. "So, boys messing with my daughter. Shall I get out the big stick?"

Sarah shrugged. "We both knew this day was coming, but it's much too soon."

"I told you not to mention the president," Jason said, unable to suppress a grin.

* * *

The situation with Julia continued to deteriorate through the following week. Every time the subject of the award ceremony was broached, she became more withdrawn.

On Wednesday morning, Jason, Jeremy and Paige sat at the table, each eating a different brand of cereal while Julia stood alone next to the island, scowling and gnawing on a breakfast bar.

"*Ta-da!*" With a flourish of scarlet and gold, Sarah burst into the kitchen wearing a brand-new dress. "Do you like it?" she asked, breathlessly.

"Wow!" Jason exclaimed, nodding his head in admiration.

"You look great, Mom!" Paige agreed.

Jeremy whistled.

Julia remained silent, but her silence was largely ignored by the others.

Later that evening, Jason knocked on his oldest daughter's bedroom door. "Jules?" he called, leaning heavily against the frame. She had retreated to her room immediately upon returning home from school and had only come out for dinner. "I'm coming in, okay?"

He pushed open the door and walked into the room. Just like the last time he had been in there, his daughter lay on her bed, her eyes staring blankly at the ceiling. A man who generally learned from experience, Jason reached out and turned off the small iPod attached to her hip before sitting down in the chair next to the bed.

"I've been doing a lot of thinking," he said, "and there's something I'd like to tell you. It was pretty clear that you weren't happy with me when you first heard about the award ceremony, but your mother and I thought you were just . . . just making a point." Julia said nothing.

"But it's obvious that something is really bothering you . . . you know, deep down," he hesitated. "So, I've decided not to go. Your mother and I are going to stay home this weekend and we'd really appreciate it if you'd think about letting us know what's been bothering you—when you're ready. Okay?"

Jason patted his daughter's leg and was about to get up out of the chair and leave when her eyes swiveled to meet his. To his great surprise, her eyes were brimming with genuine concern.

"Daddy," she said, sitting up, "you have to go."

"Don't worry, Jules," Jason answered with a reassuring smile. "It's really not a big deal to me, you know? I just want to figure out what I've done to hurt you so badly."

"You haven't done anything," she answered, her eyes beginning to glisten with moisture. "I promise, Daddy. You have to go!"

"But, honey . . ."

She took his hand and looked up at him, almost pleading now. There was a needy edge to her voice—almost panic. "Please, Daddy," she whined, "I'm sorry I've been so mean to everyone. I don't know what was the matter, but I promise its okay now and I really, really want you to go!"

Jason was feeling thoroughly confused. His instinct told him to stick with his guns and abide by the decision he and Sarah had made earlier, but one look in his daughter's mournful, pleading face melted away his determination.

"Okay," he said, "but you have to promise me that you'll let me know what's been on your mind whenever you feel up to it, okay?"

"I promise, Daddy! Thank you, thank you!"

Feeling utterly bewildered, Jason rambled down the stairs and wandered into the kitchen to tell his wife about their daughter's unusual change of heart. She was sitting at the dining room table eating cookie dough, her shoulders hunched together with anxiety.

"Well?" she breathed when he had plopped down beside her. "What happened? What did she say?"

Jason looked at Sarah for a moment and then smiled. "It was the strangest thing . . ."

* * *

On Friday afternoon, Jason came home from work early to help Sarah prepare for the trip. They spent the next several hours together—packing, laughing, cuddling, smiling and packing some more. By the time Jason had carried the last bag down and plopped it in the trunk with the others, Julia came flying by.

"Whoa! Hang on there." Jason called out. "Where are you going, young lady?"

"Oh, Dad," Julia gushed. "I'm going to Cassidy's house for a few hours. I'll be back before curfew tonight."

"Yeah, but your mother and I will be on our way to St. Louis."

The statement caused her to hesitate, spin around and return for a big hug. She mounted her bike and rode hard for the end of the block. Jason continued to stare down the now-empty street, wondering what the whirlwind was all about.

Later that evening, after helping Grandma settle in, Jason strolled to the kitchen to grab a couple bottles of water for the trip. He noticed Sarah and Paige seated at the kitchen table. Sarah looked surprisingly serious, and Paige was hunched over in her chair with her head down, almost in shame.

"What's going on?" Jason asked.

His wife looked up at him with a half smile. "Paige has something she wants to tell us, but she's a little nervous."

Curious, Jason took a seat opposite his wife and placed a reassuring hand on his daughter's shoulder. "What is it, sweetheart?" he asked.

"Honey," Sarah said, "if you think Julia might be in trouble, or is going to do something dangerous, I think you should tell us." Jason nodded in agreement, giving his daughter's arm another encouraging squeeze.

Tears welled up in her eyes as she confessed that she had eavesdropped on Julia's phone conversation with Jimmy the night before. She looked back and forth between her parents and then blurted, "She's going to a Pharm party!"

The words meant nothing to Jason, but Sarah's face went white. "What?" she gasped. "Is that what she said to Jimmy?"

Paige shook her head. "Yeah. She and her friend Cassidy are going to Jimmy's house and his dad and mom are gone tonight."

"Wait a minute," Jason broke in. "What kind of party is this? Are they cow-tipping or something?"

"No, Jason," Sarah answered, impatiently. "It's a *Pharm* party . . . P-H-A-R-M, as in *pharmaceuticals*. I read about them in *Christianity Today*. Everyone brings some kind of prescription drug to the party, and they dump the whole mess into a big bowl. Then the teens just grab handfuls of pills and pop them with alcohol."

"No," Jason said, shaking his head back and forth. "I don't think Julia could get involved with something like . . ." he stopped. All the color drained from his face.

"What?" Sarah asked.

"I had a bottle of Darvocet left over from my knee surgery a year ago," he said. "It's been in the back of our medicine cabinet ever since—just in case. But yesterday it was gone. I just figured you threw it out because it was old, but . . ." He couldn't bring himself to finish the thought.

Sarah took a deep breath, steadying herself. "What do we do?" she asked.

Jason narrowed his eyes. "I'm going to find her," he said, hopping to his feet and pulling out his car keys.

"Oh, Jason," Sarah moaned. "What about the award ceremony? The train leaves in an hour, and there aren't any more going to St. Louis tonight—I checked."

"Sarah . . . this is much more important. Don't you think?"

"I do."

"Then I need you to get on the phone with the parents of Julia's friends to see if they know anything about a party tonight." He thought for a moment, then added, "I'll start at the school and see if there are any kids still there who might know anything. Call me on my cell once you get an address."

As Jason closed the car door, he noticed a small, flat box resting on the passenger seat. He paused and then picked it up. After rotating it around in his hands for a few seconds, he pulled out the shiny medallion and held it in front of his face. The word "Hero" glinted brightly in the broad shaft of light streaming out through the screen door. With a quick shake of his head, Jason stuffed the award back in its box and drove into the night in search of his prodigal daughter.

As the shadows of the Midwest twilight deepened into evening, Jason parked his Accord at the end of a long line of cars huddled on the side of a suburban street. After a desperate hour's worth of phone calls to the parents of Julia's various acquaintances, Sarah had managed to provide him with an address. He walked swiftly to the front door of the house in question and closed his eyes, crying out to God in anguish before extending his fist and knocking loudly three times. After several minutes of listening to the muffled sounds of young, shrill voices and strange music, he tightened his hand into a fist and banged harder.

At length, the door finally opened, tripling the volume of the weird, thrumming song playing inside. A tall, scrawny teen peeked out through the opening. His jet black hair spiked away from his scalp at odd angles, and two silver rings glinted from the corner of each lip.

"Yeah? Whaddya want, old man?" he sneered, looking up at Jason with half-glazed eyes.

"I'm here to pick up my daughter," Jason answered. "Her name is Julia Millstone."

"Never heard of her," replied the youth, his lip curling up in disdain. He moved to close the door and retreat back into the thumping den, but Jason stuck out his hand and pushed back just hard enough to keep it open.

"Would you mind if I had a look around to find her?" he asked.

"Yeah, I mind," snapped the boy. Obscenities began to roll off his tongue.

Jason felt the old, familiar fog of rage begin to gather at the corners of his mind. For all he knew, this could be the same punk that had lured his daughter into this den of iniquity. *Is your name Jimmy?* He thought. But just as the fog began to reach its red, pulsing peak, he resisted. *Stay calm for Julia,* he thought. *Let's just get her and go.*

"Maybe you'd reconsider if I told you my secret."

The teen took a half step forward. "Yeah? What secret?" he asked, leaning toward Jason in order to get a better look at his face.

"Well," Jason said, "it's just that I called the police to report your little Pharm party here, and I thought you'd like to know." This was not exactly true. Jason did fully intend to alert the police about the party, but not until after he had retrieved his little girl.

"You called the cops?" the boy slurred, his eyes clearing a little bit to reveal an undercurrent of alarm.

Jason grinned, but said nothing. "Can I come in?" he asked.

The door slammed in his face. From behind it, Jason could hear the music stop suddenly, followed by the scrawny kids' muffled cry. "Hey! Hey! Some guy out there called the cops!"

The effect of his words was instantaneous. The sounds of chaos erupted as bewildered teens rushed for the door. The scuffle of feet began to crescendo toward him. The door opened and a throng of pathetic teenagers threw themselves out onto the lawn and down the street in an attempt to outrun the law.

Julia's friend Cassidy got a glimpse of Jason as she exited the house. She made a quick U-turn in the yard and ran back to the porch to shriek, "Mr. Millstone, Julia is in the house and they won't let her out!"

That was it for Jason. Not one more word was necessary. He raced into the house, knocking down several wobbly stoners still trying to get out. An instant later he had the first scrawny punk by the spiky hair of his head, stretched out over the top of a couch.

"You have five seconds to tell me where my daughter is!"

No longer able to speak, the boy pointed toward a closed door off the den. Jason pounced on the door, only to find it locked. Jason was in no mood to ask for a key, and a second later the door jam disintegrated with wood pieces flying through the air. His precious Julia needed him.

In the corner of the dimly lit room, Julia sat with her back to the wall, arms wrapped tightly around her folded legs. A young man in short pants and no shirt stood over her. In one hand he gripped her hair and in the other he held some pills.

It was obvious that his conversation with Julia had gone long past sweet-talk. He was in a rage. Julia was hysterical. And Jason—father of one wayward Julia—suddenly became young Jimmy's worst nightmare.

"Hey!" Jason shouted.

Jimmy turned to face the open doorway and owner of the voice. His eyes opened momentarily in surprise and then slowly narrowed into evil slits. He released Julia's hair, dropped the pills and rushed at Jason.

Jimmy's wild opening jab found only air as Jason delivered a powerful blow to his solar plexus. Out came the air. Off went the lights.

"Jules," Jason gasped.

His baby looked up, her face glowing white and scared. "Daddy," she whispered, getting shakily to her feet.

He pulled her into his arms, breathing hard and crying and laughing all at the same time. "You're okay," he panted. "You're okay. Thank God I found you."

"I didn't like it, Daddy. They lied to me. They trapped me."

"It's okay," he replied, wiping his eyes and wrapping his jacket around her shoulders. "We'll go back together."

The police arrived as Jason and Julia stepped slowly out onto the porch.

"Officer, you will find a young man out cold in one of the rooms. He made the mistake of attacking both me and my daughter."

As Jason drove home, he looked over at Julia's face every few moments. It was heavy and sad, weighed down by the burden of shame. Yet it was the face of a little girl who badly needed her daddy to read her a story and put her to bed.

After pulling into the garage, he unbuckled his seatbelt and began to hop out of the car, but stopped when he felt his daughter's hand on his arm. Looking over, he saw she was looking up at him, her eyes big and round and wet with tears.

"Are you disappointed in me?" she asked, her voice quivering with emotion.

Jason sighed. "Want to know what I'm really disappointed about? I'm disappointed about what's happened to our relationship," he said, gently moving a stray lock of hair away from her face. "I'm disappointed that I haven't been the kind of father you need."

She sniffed and wiped the back of her sleeve across her eyes, but said nothing.

Jason continued, placing his hand underneath his daughter's chin and lifting her eyes back to meet his own. "I'm also thrilled! I've been learning a lot about myself recently. I had no idea how far I'd fallen away from the father I wanted to be. Think you can find it in your heart to give me another try at being a good father?"

Julia sniffed again. "All this Jesus and God stuff you've been talking about for the last month," she said. "You really think it's true?"

Jason nodded. "I do, Julia. For the first time in my life, I *know* it's true."

She smiled and wiped her eyes again. "Wanna tell me about it again?"

Jason's heart almost burst to hear the words. "Yes, Jules," he said, now wiping his own eyes. "More than anything else in the world."

And he did. Jason Millstone received a divine privilege that very night. With the Scriptures in his hand, he led Julia, his eldest daughter, to Jesus.

* * *

Jason and Sarah missed their opportunity to meet the president of the United States. They chose to spend Saturday together as a family, rejoicing with Julia. She would need their nurturing love for the journey ahead.

Word of Julia's escapade and Jason's rescue reached Pastor David in the middle of the afternoon. He made a beeline for the Millstone house and was surprised to see the entire family on the back patio, comically recounting their Fiji adventures to several neighbors.

After their friends had departed, Pastor David asked them to do something they had never done before. The next evening, Jason, Sarah and their three children stood nervously before the Midland Church congregation during the Sunday evening service.

"You see," Jason continued as he leaned into the microphone, "I deeply desired to be a godly father, but I never knew what 'a godly father' really looked like. Over time, I became distracted and allowed everything else to take precedence over my own children's spiritual growth. Somehow I blamed or justified my way through each conflict and failure. My eyes became spiritually dim, and my heart was divided. I left my first love, much like the church in Ephesus."

Jason glanced over at Sarah, his eyebrows raised as if to say, *A little help from my beloved?* Without hesitation, she stepped forward and spoke.

"We went to Fiji on a family adventure, but God gave us a typhoon and the spiritual journey of a lifetime." Sarah went on to describe the *Tui Tui*, their rock of deliverance and a village full of people in need of a helping hand. The audience remained spellbound as Sarah transitioned back to Jason, who continued his side of the story.

"I met a *Tala Tala*—a Fijian pastor—who showed me God's plan for His children when they become parents." He produced the cup Pastor Jokini had used as his object lesson back in the village. With great care, Jason went on to teach the church the three principles of biblical parenting from Deuteronomy.

The people of the congregation dabbed the corners of their eyes as Jason and Sarah brought their family story to a close. Hope was born in the hearts of more than one father and mother that evening. Pastor David could not remember when so many people had hung around so late after a service. A fire had been lit in the hearts of his congregation, and David realized that it was high time for the church to build a bridge to dads and moms and the children who had been placed in their care.

As the Millstones walked together across the church parking lot, Julia clung to Jason's arm. She looked up to her father, her heavenly-appointed spiritual mentor, her eyes once again soaked with emotion.

"Dad, you are my hero!"

PART II

THE MOSES MODEL

BIBLICAL PARENTING

Why is it that most parents feel underprepared for and unequal to the task of becoming spiritual mentors to their kids? The reason has everything to do with cultural values.

How many of us while growing up attended school in order to prepare for our careers or occupations? The answer: All of us. At least twelve years for most, sixteen to eighteen for many, and more for those who have not figured how to get out of school and get on with life! What we can conclude? Inclusion into society's workforce is so important that we spend a sizeable portion of our lives preparing for it.

Yet how many of us spend even one year training to become good parents? The answer: Probably none. Not one year. Not one month. Probably not even one day. What can we conclude? The role of being a parent is so unimportant to us that preparation is unnecessary.

Is this true? If not, why do we fail to prepare?

Who Influences Whom?

Sunday School was begun more than one hundred and fifty years ago in London, England, to address the spiritual needs of children, especially unchurched boys and girls. When it began, no one thought that Sunday School and church programs should take the place of the spiritual instruction that only parents can give, which is mandated by God. Unfortunately for us in the United States, due to cultural shifts and the advent of secular humanism into the American mainstream, a subtle change in perspective began to take place. The role of Christian parents as their children's spiritual mentors gradually diminished.

The day came when well-intentioned parents started to assign their children's spiritual and moral development to the church. Please don't be hard on them! Good parenting, as Jason and Sarah Millstone discovered, is complicated and difficult on many levels. What are a father and mother to do? Delegate—hand the kids over to the church! Isn't that reasonable? Countless levelheaded parents have come to the conclusion that because their own spiritual formation happened primarily at church, why shouldn't the church take care of their kids, too?

Although such thinking is sincere in its motivation, it has proved disastrous. Rather than forfeiting yet another generation to underdeveloped biblical knowledge and shallow spirituality, the time has come to get back into the Word of God, where a priceless strategy for successful parenting was handed down long ago.

Please understand: Parents *do* need help from the church. Not as a surrogate parent to free dads and moms from their duties, but as a partner fully dedicated to leading and serving parents. Many times, however, when the opportunity has presented itself to the church to push back and say to sincere dads and moms, "The church cannot possibly bring about in your child's life what God Himself has divinely appointed you as parents to accomplish," many church leaders have said, "Okay, we'll do our best."

Imagine a church that refuses to let parents drop their kids off at the doorstep, but instead makes every effort to teach, inspire, equip, empower and ultimately send those parents into their homes to serve as their children's spiritual mentors and moral guides. Imagine a couple with a child (or two or five) who desires to raise up spiritual champions *at home* yet fully integrate them into the ministry of their church.

This church and these parents are not just figments of the imagination. They can become a reality.

Where Should We Begin?

Why not begin with the Bible? Let's take a closer look at God's plan for parents. The words of Moses in Deuteronomy 6:5-9 form the foundation and framework for every family. I call it "The Moses Model," and it's just as sound today as it was when Moses first gave it to the parents of Israel:

> You shall love the LORD your God with all your heart, with all your soul, and with all your strength. And these words which I command you today shall be in your heart. You shall teach them diligently to your children, and shall talk of them when you sit in your house, when you walk by the way, when you lie down, and when you rise up. You shall bind them as a sign on your hand, and they shall be as frontlets between your eyes. You shall write them on the doorposts of your house and on your gates.

> Love God. Obey God. Train your children.

LOVE GOD

———

Loving God is the biblical foundation for all relationships. There is no greater calling. The apostle Paul passionately beseeched his friends in Ephesus to love Jesus Christ:

> That you, being rooted and grounded in love, may be able to comprehend with all the saints what is the width and length and depth and height—to know the love of Christ which passes knowledge; that you may be filled with all the fullness of God (Eph. 3:17-19).

What must our greatest priority be for life? *To know the love of Christ.* Some may argue that God's love is unknowable because it "passes knowledge." On the contrary, Paul underscores the value in pursuing this astonishing love as life's greatest quest. Yes, God's love is so vast that we could exhaust a lifetime gathering every facet, every nugget of understanding, but there is immeasurable joy awaiting each person who answers the divine calling to know the love of God.

Faith goes beyond cerebral recognition and opens the door of the heart to Jesus Himself. It is at this heart level that the believer must be deeply rooted or, better yet, firmly established in His love. Oh, to fully comprehend the gift of Christ to humanity as the measure of God's love!

Faith and Love

Faith and love go together. If someone asked me, "What is your first priority as a Christian?" my immediate response would be, "To love God with all my heart, mind and strength." But what if the next question was, "Can you show me what that looks like?" My tendency would be to look within myself. What am I doing to prove my love? What good and noble works have I performed today? I would then go on to measure and compare those works with others. Small wonder someone once said that we are all a bunch of Pharisees in various stages of recovery!

Christ is not after my good works. He desires a surrendered heart that can be filled with His love. The outpouring of a love-filled heart will be righteous actions that bring glory to God. In other words, He will do His good work in and through me if I love Him deeply enough to relinquish control.

Paul drives this home again and again. Acting in faith is not the works I seek to perform for God to earn His favor, but my heart filled with God's love. To succeed—as Paul said—is to be filled "with all the fullness of God." To fail is to allow Satan and his followers to influence and corrupt with his evil intentions.

Flesh and Spirit

In Galatians 5:19-23, Paul compares the flesh and the Spirit. Using trees as his object lesson, he declares that a world of differences exists between the two: While the flesh produces evil works, the Spirit produces wholesome fruit. Notice the word choice: *works* of the flesh compared to *fruit* of the Spirit.

Fruit reveals God as our source. When our heart is filled with God's love, the Holy Spirit takes control. Good fruit springs forth in words and actions as the result of this loving relationship. Loving God is impossible to do in our own strength and in our own way. We must begin to love God by learning about Jesus Christ and His unconditional sacrifice for us on the cross. As we dwell on His magnificent love, our heart begins its journey of awe and gratitude. Step by step, the Holy Spirit fills our heart with an unquenchable thirst for knowing and loving God.

It stands to reason that in order to be formed into people who love God, our children need to see us deeply in love with God. The Lord acknowledged King David as a man after His own heart. For the sake of our kids, should we be anything less?

Discussion Points

1. Loving God is the foundation on which all other relationships should be built. Why?

2. What happens when we grow in our understanding of the love of Christ?

3. Read Galatians 5:19-23 and evaluate closely the nine characteristics of a Spirit-controlled Christian. How are you doing with each?

OBEY GOD

—————

Defining "love" in our culture is like trying to nail Jell-O to the wall. The average person fumbles for the right word or phrase when asked to explain what love really means.

Not so with the Bible. God's love for mankind and for His Son Jesus is demonstrated in Scripture and stands in stark contrast to the world's version. God's love is passionate, but it differs from a human feelings-based emotion. Far outstripping sentiment and passion that changes with the tides, God's love is ultimately expressed through the gift of His own Son. The apostle John wrote it this way:

> In this the love of God was manifested toward us, that God has sent His only begotten Son into the world, that we might live through Him. In this is love, not that we loved God, but that He loved us and sent His Son to be the propitiation for our sins (1 John 4:9-10).

> If you love Me, keep My commandments (John 14:15).

> He who has My commandments and keeps them, it is he who loves Me. And he who loves Me will be loved by My Father, and I will love him and manifest Myself to him (John 14:21).

If anyone loves Me, he will keep My word; and My Father will love him, and We will come to him and make Our home with him (John 14:23).

But whoever keeps his word, truly the love of God is perfected in him. By this we know that we are in Him. He who says he abides in Him ought himself also to walk just as He walked (1 John 2:5-6).

In these passages it is vitally important to connect four words: "commandments," "word," "keeps" and "walk."

- God's "commandments" are non-negotiable; they are not suggestions.
- His "word" is His will, both in spirit and letter.
- "To keep" means to observe, conform to, align with and belong to.
- To "walk" means to follow Jesus at all times.

How do we express love to God? We express our love by placing Him at the center of all that we are and hope to be and by obeying Him unreservedly. What do we obey? His commandments!

This begins with a confession that God's standards are true and good and that we have failed to live up to them (see 1 John 1:19). It grows within us as we become familiar with the clear and plain teachings of Jesus and the apostle Paul and implement those teachings into our lives. And it fully blossoms in time as we allow our minds to be conformed to Christ and His unspoken desires become our own (see Rom. 12:2).

As parents, we are responsible to God for the spiritual and moral shaping of our children. They need to see us in love with God. They need to see us in love with our spouse. Loving God

is first, last and everything in between, but the authenticity of
our love for God is routinely tested in our love for our husband
or wife. It is not surprising that loving our spouse creates a difficult but necessary inner conflict between the real us (self-
seeking and prideful) and the Spirit of God who now exercises
His rightful ownership over our lives.

We may be able to publicly disguise a feeble walk with God,
but home is a different story.

Heirs Together

Husbands, likewise, dwell with [your wives] with understanding, giving honor to the wife, as to the weaker vessel, and as being heirs together of the grace of life, that
your prayers may not be hindered (1 Pet. 3:7).

The apostle Peter explained this God-ordained marriage relationship as "heirs together of the grace of life." Sounds exciting—because it *is* exciting! Let's look at this a bit more closely.

- *Heirs:* beneficiaries, recipients, those who have or will
  inherit something
- *Together:* jointly, as one, simultaneously
- *Of the grace:* of the unmerited favor, benevolence, kindness
- *Of life:* of existence, being, quality of life

Putting this all together, we can rest assured that God has
special plans for husbands and wives. By the way, "weaker vessel" does not imply mental, moral, spiritual or any other kind
of inferiority. The implication of this word picture is physical
and it points to the beautiful femininity and delicacy of a
woman as she is lifted high in honor by her husband.

How Much Love?

Husbands, love your wives, just as Christ also loved the church and gave Himself for her, that He might sanctify and cleanse her with the washing of water by the word, that He might present her to Himself a glorious church, not having spot or wrinkle or any such thing, but that she should be holy and without blemish (Eph. 5:25-27).

Husbands, how much love are we talking about? Nothing less than sacrificial love. Now, by "sacrificial," I don't mean that you should go out and kill yourself to prove you love your wife (that would be terribly selfish!) but that you should try to love her each and every day with abandon. Buying a bouquet of flowers because you were insensitive might be a good start, but what she's really looking for is daily affirmation, attentiveness and care.

Start with saying no to self and yes to your wife where there is a conflict of interest. Even better, try to anticipate what her day was like, and then talk to her about it. Or find out something that she likes and enjoy it with her—even if it's not your favorite thing to do. The key here is to put *her* needs first, ahead of your own.

Do your children need to see Mom and Dad honoring and loving one another? Of course they do! When children see their parents faithfully loving and obeying God, they see truth on display. When they see their parents faithfully loving each other, they live in a sanctuary of trust and safety. Truth and trust are very effective tools in opening children's hearts to God.

How will they see all this?

It all goes back to the beginning of this study: when they watch you obeying God's commandments, keeping His Word and walking with Jesus.

Discussion Points

1. God revealed His love for us by giving His only Son. What is the greatest expression of our love we can give in return? Explain.

2. How is it possible for us to walk as Jesus walked?

3. What will be the effect on our children when they see us love and obey God?

4. What will be the effect on our children when they see us love each other?

5. Where should husbands begin in learning to love their wives sacrificially?

LESSON 3

TRAIN YOUR CHILDREN

———

I once met a lady who was hostile toward any form of spiritual training for her children. Her words to me in my office went something like this: "I will certainly not force my children into religious beliefs. It is much better to wait until they are older so that they can decide for themselves!"

I asked her a question: "So . . . you don't make them brush their teeth?"

Our conversation quickly got to the real issue: values. To her, training her children in spiritual matters was of no value, while training them to brush their teeth was high priority—in fact, she made them brush twice daily! She did not realize that, in the same way that teeth begin to decay if they are not cared for early and properly, the lives of children begin to decay if they are not mentored to love God and follow Jesus.

The primary mentors for the lives of children are their parents. The Lord never instructed or empowered the Church to spiritually train children apart from parents. Nor did He expect parents to train their children in complete isolation from the Church. A suitable partnership is waiting for pastors and parents who are willing to wrestle with God's Word and its implications. There is a potential spiritual treasure buried in the lives of children, and it can be discovered only when they grow up under the watchful, loving eyes of dads and moms deeply in love with Jesus. May the Lord reach the hearts of this generation of parents!

The Mandate

The God-given mandate to parents is to train up children in the way they should go. Parents are commissioned to mentor their children to become lovers of God and followers of Jesus. The seriousness of this undertaking cannot be overstated.

The Example

Parents must lead first by example. Hypocrisy at home never brings the desired outcome. Children need their parents' best—and the best begins with loving God and ends with the commitment to follow Jesus. Consider Joseph and Mary:

> So when they had performed all things according to the law of the Lord, they returned to Galilee, to their own city, Nazareth. And the Child grew and became strong in spirit, filled with wisdom; and the grace of God was upon Him (Luke 2:39-40).

The Timing

When should parents start training children to walk in the ways of the Lord? Early! Paul recognized the blessing of early training in young Timothy's life.

> But you must continue in the things which you have learned and been assured of, knowing from whom you have learned them, and that from childhood you have known the Holy Scriptures, which are able to make you wise for salvation through faith which is in Christ Jesus (2 Tim. 3:15).

The Model

Again, this all begins by loving God with your whole being: "Love the Lord your God with all your heart, with all your soul, and with all your strength" (Deut. 6:8). When you love God, you will express that love by obeying Him unreservedly: "If anyone loves Me, he will keep My word; and My Father will love him, and We will come to him and make Our home with him" (John 14:23). And it is modeled when you train your children to follow the Word of God: "Teach [the word of the Lord] diligently to your children . . . when you sit in your house, when you walk by the way, when you lie down, and when you rise up" (Deut. 6:7).

Love God. Obey God. Train your children.